The Future of the Soviet Economy: 1978-1985

Other Titles in This Series

Westview Special Studies on the Soviet Union and Eastern Europe

The Future of the Soviet Economy: 1978-1985
edited by Holland Hunter

Where will the Soviet economy be heading in the 1980s? How is the economy likely to react to slowed growth in the labor force and increased pressure for supplies of energy and raw materials? This volume, growing out of papers prepared for the October 1977 national conference of the American Association for the Advancement of Slavic Studies, offers an integrated exposition of these issues. The authors use historical evidence and macroeconometric models of the Soviet economy as bases from which to view the future, assessing the possible results of the interaction between Soviet policy and potential developments.

Holland Hunter is professor of economics and chairman of the Economics Department at Haverford College. He is also senior consultant to the Strategic Studies Center of SRI-International. His analyses of the Soviet economy have appeared in numerous books and articles and in the compendia issued in 1959, 1966, 1969, and 1976 by the Joint Economic Committee of Congress on the Soviet economy.

The Future of the Soviet Economy: 1978-1985

edited by Holland Hunter

Contributors:
David W. Carey
Daniel Gallik
Donald W. Green
Philip Grossman
Daniel R. Kazmer
Barbara S. Severin
F. Douglas Whitehouse

Westview Press / Boulder, Colorado

Westview Special Studies
on the Soviet Union and Eastern Europe

Copyright © 1978 by Westview Press, Inc.

Published in 1978 in the United States of America by
    Westview Press, Inc.
    5500 Central Avenue
    Boulder, Colorado 80301
    Frederick A. Praeger, Publisher

Library of Congress Catalog Card Number: 78-7150
ISBN: 0-89158-097-2

Printed and bound in the United States of America

CONTENTS

TABLES

FIGURES

PREFACE

This joint enterprise began as a session at the October 1977 national convention of the American Association for the Advancement of Slavic Studies. The panel discussion was organized under the leadership of John P. Hardt, Congressional Research Service, Library of Congress. The participants agreed to convert their compact reports into chapters in a book designed to provide a balanced evaluation of current prospects for the Soviet economy. Though all the authors carry heavy responsibilities in their respective organizations, they agreed to revise and augment their papers within three months. The Westview Press in turn offered unusually prompt production of a book using camera-ready copy. We thus sought to avoid the long delays that often afflict the published outcomes of scholarly meetings. Slight slippage in deadlines has enabled us to incorporate evidence up through the end of February, 1978.

The analysis in this book is based on primary evidence, mainly in published Soviet books and periodicals. Footnotes provide selected references at key points and also suggest a few supplementary or alternative treatments. The views expressed in the chapters represent the opinions of the respective authors and do not necessarily reflect the views of their organizations. Most of the referenced sources are readily available. Working papers relating to SOVMOD, the SRI-WEFA macroeconometric model of the Soviet economy, are available from SRI International, 1611 North Kent Street, Arlington, VA 22209. The cited reports issued by the Office of Economic Research, Central Intelligence Agency, are available from Photoduplication Service, Library of Congress, Washington, D.C. 20540.

As editor I acknowledge with gratitude the equanimity of the principal authors as they responded quite flexibly to suggestions for prompt changes. We are all especially grateful for the precision and craftsmanship displayed by Linda Langley in preparing the camera-ready copy.

HOLLAND HUNTER

1
INTRODUCTION
Holland Hunter
Haverford College

This book is an effort to assess the Soviet midterm economic future. Some will feel the effort itself is doubtful. Assessing the future is even harder than assessing the past. Prudence has traditionally suggested that one should wait for the dust to settle before evaluating complex situations. But today's decisions require judgments concerning prospective developments, and cautious decision makers can benefit from systematic efforts to review plausible future possibilities. It is in this spirit that the following analyses are offered.

Assessment of future possibilities is gaining in rigor as new techniques make it possible to ask and answer future-oriented questions with greater precision. The analyses in this book reflect the use of powerful new methods. They rest, first of all, on a painstakingly assembled base of quantitative evidence covering the last 20 years. They make use, secondly, of quantitative models of the Soviet economy. Disaggregated models of an economy, like those in this book, have several marked advantages:

- They enforce simultaneous attention to all major aspects of the interrelated stocks and flows of economic activity;

- They demand consistency among these parts as they evolve over time; and

- They permit experimentation: hypothetical changes can be introduced into the model, and their impact can be traced throughout the economy and into subsequent periods.

Economic modeling therefore provides an orderly framework in which to conduct cautious forays into the future. The forays are disciplined by the economy's structural inheritance and

1

constrained by the economy's short-run technological rigidities. Numerous independent assumptions can be linked logically within a framework that tests for consistency and feasibility. A detailed and flexible extension of the present into the future becomes possible.(1)

In this book we do not present single-valued predictions about the Soviet economic future. We offer instead a systematic preview of plausible outcomes generated by alternative possibilities over the next five or ten years. The possibilities are of two kinds. First there are the objective factors that will condition Soviet economic activity, such as the weather, the availability of fuels and raw materials, the size and composition of the population, and the structure of world trade. Alternative prospects here have been specified, and potential trends have been spelled out in some detail. Secondly, there are the behavioral responses that can be made by Soviet authorities, Soviet consumers, and all those engaged in Soviet economic activities. Here too the analyst can propose any number of well-specified assumptions and investigate the consequences for the economy if the responses occur.

As the analyst traces the outcomes generated by alternative assumptions, concerning both the objective factors and the behavioral responses, he produces a number of scenarios, each one a case study placed in the future. It is neither necessary nor desirable to reject all but the one scenario considered most likely to occur. The full set becomes an avenue to improved understanding. The testing process itself builds up a valuable body of future-oriented, yet empirical, evidence concerning the structure and properties of the economy being studied. One develops an appreciation of its contours, of its points of flexibility and rigidity. Having canvassed a wide variety of hypothetical challenges and responses, one emerges with an almost clinical feel for the economy's range of sensitivity, i.e., the upper and lower limits of its plausible reactions to potential developments.

In thus assessing the future we cannot hope for tidy truths. Our goal is limited to providing "advance evidence"

----

(1)
    For an impressive example of disaggregated, future-oriented analysis using an interindustry, intertemporal model, see Clopper Almon, Jr., et al., 1985: Interindustry Forecasts of the American Economy, Lexington: D.C. Heath, 1974.

concerning a range of plausible potential developments, placed in a coherent and consistent framework. If the effort seems rash, it can be defended as a basis for improving the decisions that must be made today -- decisions whose impact will carry forward into the period we are examining. Decisions with future consequences deserve to have light thrown on the era in which those consequences will unfold. By the same token it is clear that efforts like ours are never completed. We must recognize the need for regular updating and revision of our projections. The half-life of this volume therefore may be something like two-to-four years. That is why we have sought prompt publication and express gratitude for our publisher's efficiency. That is also why we cheerfully expect rather prompt obsolescence of our insights.

THE PRESENT OUTLOOK FOR THE SOVIET ECONOMY

The Soviet GNP will grow at reduced rates in the 1980s. A gradual decline in growth rates has been evident over the past two decades and it seems clear that the trend will continue. This is not to say that the overall GNP is likely to become absolutely smaller; an impressive upward potential is still visible. It does seem clear, however, that the rate of overall expansion in output is likely to be modest during the 1980s, especially in comparison with the rapid growth rates of the past.

Another major feature of the Soviet economy in the 1980s will be the growing pressure of burgeoning demands on Soviet energy supplies. The USSR contains massive energy resources, and during the 1980's they will be drawn on to support the domestic economy, to supply the needs of Eastern Europe, and to earn hard currency abroad. But these demands in the aggregate will increasingly strain short-run availabilities. In addition, the outlook for bringing new deposits into production five or ten years from now is distinctly unfavorable. Extraction costs are rising and the threat of real shortages is visible on the horizon.

During the 1980s shortages of labor will be a serious problem. The cohorts of young men and women entering the labor force will be substantially smaller in the mid-eighties than they have been over the last two decades, while there will also be substantial exits from the labor force as large cohorts retire. Moreover, the regional availabilities of labor will not match up well with the geographic pattern of demands for labor as presently foreseen.

The strains generated by interaction between the state's demands for continued growth, on the one hand, and constrained

additional suppplies of energy and labor, on the other, extend
also into the agricultural sector, the defense sector, and
Soviet external economic relations. Soviet state farms and
collective farms currently absorb very large flows of current
inputs without producing an adequate flow of output.
Institutional malfunctioning prevents efficient performance in
Soviet agriculture. The Soviet defense sector, by contrast,
appears to be turning out an impressive flow of national
defense services, drawing on the best resources the economy
can provide. In both areas, however, some specific policy
changes could have the effect of releasing a substantial
volume of resources and thus relieving some of the strains on
tight labor and energy supplies. Soviet foreign trade presents
still another prospect -- that of a more marginal factor
without much capacity to relieve strains in the 1980s.

What is the detailed evidence that leads to these
expectations? In the chapters that follow, seven knowledgeable
students of the Soviet economy set forth the underlying
statistical and other evidence, evaluate its solidity, and
reflect on its implications. While the book does not analyze
every aspect of the Soviet economy, it does scrutinize the
major factors that will shape overall trends. These analyses
also give considerable attention to the likely direction of
Soviet responses to key economic problems. On the basis of
past policies and current Soviet discussion of plans and
intentions, a number of alternative Soviet policy directions
are specified and investigated.

Interacting with the underlying trends in resource
availabilities, the alternative policies generate alternative
expansion paths with distinctively different contents. Each
expansion-path outcome incorporates detailed answers to
"what-if" questions that have been phrased with great
specificity. Users of our results will thus be able to select
the variants most appropriate for their needs. As actual
events preempt the field of our assumptions, many of the
possibilities previously entertained will be closed off. By
the same token other scenarios will become more likely, and
needed revisions will become more obvious. If subsequent
analyses are facilitated by our current efforts, we will feel
that our attempt in 1978 to assess the Soviet economy in the
1980s has made a worthwhile contribution.

RATIONALE AND PLAN OF THE BOOK

A study of this kind faces an optimization problem in
relation to extent of coverage and selection of topics.
Detailed and exhaustive analysis, however desirable in
principle, nevertheless is constrained by capacity limits in

staffing, in available time, and in publisher's hospitality. My co-authors and I would have welcomed attention to several aspects of the Soviet economy that are slighted here: the construction sector, transport and communications, regional trends, the second economy, and others. Within existing limitations, however, we have tried to identify and evaluate the key forces at work -- and the major sectoral trends reflecting them -- so that an accurate and balanced assessment of broad outcomes can emerge. As the reader will see, it is a tentative view, offered with firmness as to the implications of recent trends but readily modifiable as events unfold.

Chapter 2, "Output Trends: Prospects and Problems," takes an economywide view. It begins by noting a persistent downward trend in Soviet output growth as the basic problem to be examined. Two methodological approaches are applied to current Soviet evidence, and their implications are contrasted with Soviet output targets for the year 1980. The chapter next considers major constraints on growth during the 1980s. It examines the impact of demographic constraints, rising costs, and materials shortcomings. The role of imported technology in offsetting these constraints is evaluated. Next, some policy options in the area of investment and manpower allocation are investigated. Alternative growth paths are derived as consequences of implementing specific policies. The results of the computations are assessed as to likelihood and significance.

Chapter 3, "The USSR and the World Economy in the 1980s," begins by reviewing the major interrelationships between the domestic Soviet economy and the outside world. The current and prospective pattern of imports and exports is summarized, together with associated financial flows. Chapter 3 then employs a macroeconometric model to provide a baseline projection, year by year, of Soviet foreign trade. It incorporates existing trends and a series of assumptions tested for their plausibility and operational consistency. With this baseline solution as a reference point, three problem scenarios are investigated to see how much difference they would make for the overall economy if they occur. The implications of the exercises lead to some concluding reflections.

Chapter 4, "The Outlook for Soviet Agriculture," deals with a large and ailing sector of the economy. The authors present a careful review of actual farm and food supply conditions as they presently exist and are slated to evolve by 1980. The chapter then examines potential for greater efficiency and increased agricultural output resulting from some possible changes in the 1980s. The chapter also reviews prospects and potential strains in the interaction between

5

consumer incomes, available supplies, and consumer demands for agricultural products.

Chapter 5, "The Defense Burden and Arms Controls," presents a compact and thoughtful discussion of the subject. Its opening section notes previous attempts to measure the size of Soviet national defense efforts and the impact these efforts have on the Soviet economy. Stress is laid on the inadequacies of past efforts at measurement, and on the breadth of uncertainties of this area. The chapter then examines evidence on the perceptions of defense burden that are held in Soviet minds and notes analogous issues of burden perception in US minds. Finally, the author turns to reflecting on some implications (a) for Soviet domestic economic policy, (b) for Soviet foreign policy and arms control policy, and (c) for US responses to developments on the Soviet side.

Chapter 6, "Labor Supply Constraints and Responses," provides detailed evidence concerning a central constraint on the coming Soviet economy. It presents annual estimates for the decelerating growth of the labor force, looking separately at youthful entrants and those leaving the labor force. It offers projections of the labor force assuming unchanged participation rates. The discussion then shifts to analysis of four ways for getting more out of Soviet human resources through (a) raising the participation rate, (b) squeezing some people out of the armed forces, (c) squeezing some people out of the agricultural sector, or (d) raising the average work week. Beyond this, the chapter offers illustrative computations concerning the potential that lies in accelerated productivity growth.

Finally, the summary observations and reflections of Chapter 7 serve several ends. They enumerate the constraints on Soviet growth and outline several problems in the composition of Soviet output. In considering the prospect for improvements, the chapter then discusses a number of dilemmas confronting efforts at reform. Each chapter in the body of the book examines alternative prospects for its sector; the concluding chapter sketches two clusters of possibilities -- one assuming that the Soviet policies and economic institutions remain unchanged as they deal with current problems, the other assuming that a series of institutional reforms are carried out. The study ends with brief reflections on the significance of these alternatives for the outside world.

2

OUTPUT TRENDS: PROSPECTS
AND PROBLEMS

F. Douglas Whitehouse and Daniel R. Kazmer
Central Intelligence Agency

INTRODUCTION

In contrast to most industrially developed countries where productivity gains have been a key factor in economic growth, the USSR has relied more heavily on massive injections of labor and new fixed capital to support its growth in GNP. During the 1950s this policy resulted in rapid gains in output because of the very low level of GNP in the early post-war period and the relatively high efficiency of new fixed investment in reconstruction and repair of war damage.

As the USSR moved into the 1960s and out of the reconstruction phase, however, highly efficient investment projects became more difficult to identify and centralized planning and management of a burgeoning economy became increasingly cumbersome and inefficient. Productivity slowed, and capital-output ratios rose rapidly. Since the mid-1960s the Soviet leadership has groped continually for ways to stimulate growth in productivity. Failing this, there was little choice but to continue the large commitment of resources to investment if economic growth was to continue apace.

Thus, during the past decade, industrial and agricultural growth have been supported by average annual rates of growth in capital assets nearly 1 1/2 and 3 times their growth in output respectively. In addition to maintaining steadily larger annual flows of investment, Soviet planners have swelled the expansion of capital stocks by:

- Holding retirements of aging equipment to a minimum. On the average, the service lives of Soviet industrial assets are about twice those for comparable assets in the US.

- Prolonging the service lives of technologically obsolete capital through repeated extensive capital repairs. In the early 1970s such repairs amounted to roughly 60% of all expenditures on machinery and equipment.

- Continually expanding new construction projects, thus channeling the bulk of investment into buildings and structures rather than into new machinery and equipment, though the latter is the principal carrier of new technology.

Sustaining a high level of increase in total capital assets by these methods has impeded technological progress and productivity gains. Efforts to increase the quality and quantity of output and make better use of available resources continue to be frustrated by a backward technological base, inflexible production processes, and a cumbersome and inefficient system of planning and management.

On top of this, future Soviet attempts to halt adverse trends in output and productivity growth must overcome resource problems quite different from anything experienced since World War II. In addition to the continuation of chronic difficulties related to low efficiency, several new problems will beset the regime. The rate of growth of the labor force will decrease sharply in the early 1980s due to the decline in birth rates which occurred in the 1960s. At the same time the costs of obtaining raw materials and semi-finished goods will rise sharply, as will the demand for technologically advanced finished products. In short, the economy will be under increasing pressure to produce more and better products with declining resource increments at increasing costs. As a result, Soviet economic growth, which has been slowing gradually since the late 1950s, may continue to fall -- perhaps even more rapidly than before. In the light of historical precedent, one might expect growth to average 3% in the 1980s. Despite some large annual fluctuations, GNP growth has fallen by one percentage point on the average each decade since the 1950s.

USSR: Average Annual Rates of Growth in GNP in Percentages

1950s	1960s	1970s	1980s
6	5	4	?

Since resource availability in the USSR is likely to be more severely limited in the next decade than it ever was in the past, however, the USSR may do well just to maintain this historical trend.

It is therefore the purpose of this chapter to broadly define the growth prospects for the Soviet economy through the mid-1980s by applying a combination of econometric techniques and analytical judgments to the resource environment which Soviet growth strategists now face, and to assess the likely impact of some alternative policies that Soviet leaders might pursue.

PROJECTING SOVIET ECONOMIC GROWTH

Our analysis of Soviet economic prospects has proceeded along two separate but often intersecting paths: "traditional or conventional analysis" and use of a large simultaneously solved econometric model.

Traditional Analysis(1)

The content of "traditional or conventional analysis" is difficult to define precisely since that content will change from one application to another. In this case, the traditional approach has been based on previous trends and patterns in Soviet economic performance. Central to our analysis is the aggregate production function. In our prognosis for the USSR, both the general form and the precise characteristics of the relationship between output and inputs have been assumed or specified by analogy with Western practice.

Although a variety of production functions were investigated, the aggregate production function used in this analysis was the generally accepted Cobb-Douglas form:

$$Q = AL^b K^c D^{(1-b-c)}$$

----

(1)
Generally, this approach follows that used by Abram Bergson, "Toward a New Growth Model," Problems of Communism, March-April 1973, pp. 1-9.

9

where: Q = GNP
        L = labor in man-hours
        K = capital stock
        D = land
        A = combined factor productivity

The coefficients b, c, and (1-b-c) represent respectively the
distribution of labor costs (including wages, "other" income,
and social insurance deductions), capital costs (depreciation
and a twenty percent charge on fixed capital net of
depreciation), and land rent. These coefficients were
constrained to sum to one, so constant returns to scale were
assumed. The distribution of these factor costs in production
was derived from the 1970 GNP accounts for the Soviet
Union.(2) The shares of labor, capital, and land use were
computed at 55.8 percent, 41.2 percent, and 3.0 percent,
respectively.

The combined factor productivity term, A, is a residual
which includes all increases or decreases in production not
explained by increases or decreases in the primary inputs of
capital, labor, and land. This term incorporates new
technology, qualitative improvements in management, production
engineering, health and education of workers, and
organization, changes in output mix and material inputs, good
luck, and anything else not accounted for by quantitative
changes in the primary inputs.

For the period through 1980, our GNP forecast utilizes
Soviet planned increments to inputs and the assumption that
factor productivity will follow past trends.

Average Annual Rates of Growth of Factor Productivity
in Percentages

1951-60	1961-70	1971-75
1.2	0.8	-0.6

----

(2)

USSR: Gross National Product Accounts, 1970, CIA,
November 1975, A(ER) 75-76.

10

Since the growth of combined factor productivity is subject to variations in a large variety of factors, the forecast for GNP is given below as a range where factor productivity is allowed to vary between zero and one percent per year.

Average Annual Rates of Growth in Percentages, 1976-80
===
Combined Factor Productivity	GNP
0.0	3.5
0.5	4.0
1.0	4.5

Based on past performance, it seems likely that factor productivity will grow between zero and one half percent per year through the balance of the seventies. Thus, we expect that the average growth of GNP will not exceed 4 percent per year during this period.

In contrast to the 1976-80 period, our GNP projection for 1981-85 is based on the production function given above and the following assumptions about the growth of labor, capital, land, and factor productivity.

Labor is assumed to grow at an average annual rate of 1 percent per year. This is based on analysis of the projected demographic trends which suggest that labor force growth will exhibit a declining rate from about 1.3% per year in the early 1980s to about 0.5% per year in the mid-1980s.

The growth of capital stock is more difficult to predict because of the changing Soviet strategy for capital formation. Assuming that investment continues to grow at the relatively low rate planned for 1976-80 and that some success is achieved in reducing the growth of unfinished construction, we estimate that capital stock will growth by 5 to 5 1/2 percent per year in 1981-85 (a figure of 5.3% is used in the calculations for convenience).

The growth rate of land is arbitrarily held at 0.5% per year -- the same rate planned for 1976-80. This reflects the effect of Soviet land reclamation programs.

While factor productivity is difficult to project, we believe that the growth of factor productivity will not exceed 1% per year in 1981-85 and could even be zero or negative if

the Soviets encounter severe weather problems resulting in two
or more poor agricultural years.

Given the above assumptions the production function for
GNP yields a forecast growth range in 1981-85 as follows:

Average Annual Rates of Growth in Percentages, 1981-85

Combined Factor Productivity	GNP
0.0	2.6
0.5	3.0
1.0	3.7

A rate of 3.3% was chosen as consistent with our analysis of
the constraints on Soviet growth in 1981-85 in comparison with
the constraints on growth in previous periods.

The Modeling Approach

The second part of our analytical effort involves the use
of a large simultaneously solved econometric model of the
Soviet economy.(3) The quantity of production determines the
sector-of-origin side of GNP, part of which goes into
inventories. Production also determines wages, prices, and
incomes, which in turn interact to yield consumption.
Consumption, the state budget (including defense), investment,
inventories, and foreign trade determine end-use GNP.

The model has been exercised for two purposes, the first
of which is to provide more detailed information on specific
interactions within the economy.

In order to assess the viability of alternative Soviet
policy options for dealing with the problems discussed in this
paper several simulated economic situations (or scenarios)
were analyzed with the help of the model. Although the

----

(3)
The model is an immediate descendant of SOVMOD III, whose
first identified ancestor is fully described in Donald W.
Green and Christopher I. Higgins, SOVMOD I: A
Macroeconometric Model of the Soviet Union, Academic
Press, New York, 1977. SOVMOD III and its applications
are also discussed in Donald Green's paper elsewhere in
this volume.

simulations are hypothetical, they were designed to test the economy's response to conditions and policies that have a reasonable likelihood of occuring.

Two general conclusions emerge from the scenarios. First, the Soviet economy is so large that many shocks administered to it have surprisingly small effects on major aggregates such as GNP. Second, scenarios predicated on investment effects (such as increases in defense spending or restrictions on investment) have relatively little impact on the growth of GNP, but substantial effects on the composition of growth and, of course, on the allocation of resources. The relatively minor impact on growth occurs for two reasons:

- Investment can affect output only through its effect on capital stocks, and there is a long lag before even annually applied shocks to investment can cumulate sufficiently to alter the growth of capital stocks.

- Because the contribution of labor to output is greater than the contribution of capital in most sectors of the Soviet economy, economic aggregates will be relatively insensitive to marginal changes in investment but will be highly sensitive to marginal changes in labor supply and probably key material inputs.

One of the most difficult problems facing the leadership is the potential manpower shortage. If substantial increases in productivity are not forthcoming, the leadership will have to find other ways to augment the scheduled increases in employment or settle for very low rates of growth of output. Increasing the participation rates is not a viable option since the Soviets appear already to have pushed this source of labor to the limit. Increasing the work-week is probably also unacceptable from a political viewpoint. However, the possibility of reallocating future employment increases from sectors of relatively low priority (e.g. services) to those of higher priority (e.g. industry) may be contemplated.

If, for example, the annual increment to the share of services in nonagricultural employment in 1977-85 were transferred to the share of industrial employment, the average annual growth rate of industrial output would be about 1/2 of one percentage point higher during the period 1977-85. While the growth rate of services output would decline by about one percentage point, the GNP growth rate would increase by .2-.3 percentage points. The growth rate of consumption would also increase slightly and the composition of consumption would shift as food, soft goods and particularly durables

13

consumption accelerated to offset the lower growth rate in consumption of services.

The net effect of these changes on the economy is difficult to judge, but under ceterus paribus conditions such a reallocation of labor resources may be a very attractive option for a regime bent on maintaining relatively high rates of output growth with a declining flow of resource increments.

It is also possible that military manpower may be held at current levels instead of increasing in 1977-85. We estimate that this would free nearly a million people for reallocation to the civilian economy. If this labor were allocated to industry, the rate of growth of industrial output would increase by roughly .1-.3 percentage points during 1977-85 and the growth rate of total defense spending would decline by about .2 percentage points. The growth of GNP would only be raised marginally after 1980 (i.e., about .1 percentage point). Little or no impact would be made on investment since military procurement was not altered. The growth rate of consumption, however, would rise by about .2 percentage points during 1981-85 to absorb the additional output of the industrial sector.

The second purpose in exercising the model is to compare its aggregate projections with those arrived at by conventional analysis. The results in general corroborated the estimates presented in the preceding section. Both the conventionl analysis and the use of the model yielded projections for growth in Soviet GNP of four percent per year, 1976-80. In the latter part of this period and in the early eighties, the two approaches yield increasingly divergent projections. For 1981-85, the modeling approach projects GNP growth at four percent per year while our conventional analysis yields only three percent.

The model we exercised, like all models, is strong in some areas and weak in others. It is particularly well-suited to analysis of the two classic inputs, capital and labor. It is not well suited, however, to handling several issues which will become increasingly important in the eighties. Shortages of key material inputs including fuels and steel are not effectively analyzed since they do not enter the model's production functions as inputs. Likewise, the growing regional imbalance is not amenable to analysis through this model. Newly discovered deposits of fuels and ores are more often to be found in Siberia far from the industrial centers of European Russia. The model includes no regional breakdown. Finally, the issues of technological progress and productivity growth are not well treated in the model. Soviet success or failure to come to grips with these and other issues vital to

14

their economic growth will be decided by their investment strategy, the constraints on capital formation which may thwart that strategy, and their ability to achieve efficiency in the use of increasingly scarce and costly resources.

THE INVESTMENT STRATEGY(4)

The Soviet investment strategy through 1980 reflects the leadership's awareness of at least some impending resource constraints, as well as the difficulties of trying to cope with them within a system characterized by years of rigid resource allocation and a built-in aversion to innovation. At present the leadership is counting heavily on its ability to redirect the emphasis in capital formation away from the traditional pattern of extensive growth to one of concentration and modernization. Indeed, the main focus of capital formation during the next 5-8 years will be on the renovation and automation of existing plant and equipment -- first, by concentrating investment resources in those branches which provide the basic machinery and technologically advanced equipment for such modernization throughout the economy; second, by cutting back on the number of new construction starts, and concentrating resources on completing projects already in-train; and third, by increasing the mechanization and automation of labor-intensive auxiliary processes (such as materials handling, loading-unloading, and warehousing) which currently absorb more than one-third of the USSR's total industrial employment. In this way the leadership hopes to raise the share of machinery and equipment in total investment, upgrade the technological level of its industrial base, and raise the productivity of labor and capital resources.

Modernization

Modernization of the USSR's industrial plant hinges critically on the performance of the machinery sector -- the source of equipment for investment, defense hardware, and consumer durables. However, this sector itself must undergo substantial renovation before it can begin to turn out the

----

(4)
    Many of the points raised in this section are treated more extensively by Stanley H. Cohn, "Deficiencies in Soviet Investment Policies and the Technological Imperative," in JEC print, Soviet Economy in a New Perspective, 1976, pp. 447-459.

large quantities of high quality equipment needed to upgrade the other industrial sectors.

Machinery production currently is plagued by a technologically outdated machine tool stock. The Soviet penchant for low depreciation rates and excessive service lives has given rise to an increasing share of machine tools with rising maintenance costs and declining productivity. Not only does depreciation policy tend to disregard obsolescence, but actual retirement rates are often much lower than the designated depreciation rates. As a substitute for retirement, service lives are prolonged unduly by large annual increases in capital repair. In fact, more than one-third of all machine tools are used just to repair older machines and to produce spare parts. Historically, machine tools used for repair have been replaced more rapidly than machine tools used for production. Thus, a signficant portion of the USSR'S machine tool inventory has been condemned to relatively unproductive and inefficient use. While Soviet plans for 1980 indicate a relatively rapid rise in the output of machine tools (9% per year in value terms), some improvement in assortment and degree of specialization, and a step-up in the rate of replacement, there is no indication that any change in the pattern of use is contemplated.

Thus, the modernization of machinery will materialize only slowly. Because of the reluctance of managers to disrupt the production process, thus causing a loss of output and bonuses, heavier reliance on capital repair than on replacement is likely to continue.(5) If prolonged delays are incurred in modernizing machinery, the entire process of modernizing the economy also will be delayed, further frustrating the efforts to increase the productivity of labor and capital resources.

----

(5)
   Both capital repair and replacement require shutdown. Capital repair is less disruptive than replacement because it keeps in place a piece of equipment which has gone through its shakedown phase and has proven itself except for the recent fault to be repaired. New equipment requires an extensive shakedown phase to correct faults, repair damage in shipping and installation, and possibly removal of the equipment from the line or even the plant if problems are sufficiently serious.

Reducing Unfinished Construction

In order to maintain relatively high rates of growth in additions to new fixed capital stock in spite of a substantially lower rate of growth in investment during 1976-80, the Soviets will have to reduce sharply the chronic delays in construction and equipment installation which have led to a large and growing backlog of unfinished construction.(6) In 1975, the accumulated total of unfinished construction was equal to 75% of that year's state capital investments. The growing backlog of unfinished construction means that large quantities of investment resources are immobilized and incapable of yielding capital services. Thus, the embodiment of new technology into the production process is further delayed. Currently, construction takes so long that the embodied technology is already obsolete when production begins.(7)

As part of the investment strategy through 1980, the leadership hopes to curtail drastically the quantity of new construction starts by holding the growth of investment to only 3.2% per year compared with an average annual rate of growth of 7.0% in 1971-75. In addition, the construction sector has been admonished to concentrate on completing those projects already in-train, thus reducing the growth in the backlog of unfinished construction. If successful, this policy would lead to some one-time gains in capital formation, but the new construction starts foregone over the next few years may lead to a slowdown in capital formation in the late 1980s.

Similar campaigns have been waged in the past with mixed results. In 1973, for example, investment growth dropped

----

(6)

Unfinished construction refers to construction and installation work beyond the initial stages, but not finished to the point of permitting use of the assets. Included is equipment in the process of being installed or actually in place in uncompleted structures.

(7)

Official estimates for the mid-sixties show that the total elapsed time between project initiation and full scale production averages 7 to 8 years for large enterprises and, for some, as much as a dozen years. In 1969, first deputy chairman of the USSR State Committee on Science and Technology, V. A. Trapeznikov, identified construction delays as largely responsible for the Soviets' technological lag behind the West.

17

sharply as new construction starts were held to a minimum, thereby slowing the growth in unfinished construction. In 1974, however, the proliferation of new projects resumed and the backlog of unfinished construction shot up by more than double the 1973 increase.

The inability to hold down new starts and complete old projects is inextricably linked to the system of planning and management. Overriding concern with growth and high investment rates impels ministries and enterprises to press as many projects as possible on the planning agencies. Project completions are frustrated by endemic bottlenecks in the supply of components and a lack of incentives in construction organizations, where plan fulfillment is largely based on the value of work completed. Basic construction work is recorded at high ruble values, but finishing work is not.

Mechanization and Automation

Mechanization and automation of labor-intensive processes, especially auxiliary processes, is probably the most promising approach for raising the productivity of the USSR's industrial labor force in the next 5 years. More than half of all industrial workers in the USSR perform manual work, and this share has been declining at a snail's pace -- at the rate of about one-half a percentage point each year. Most of these workers -- 38% in the machinery sector -- are engaged in auxiliary production activities. Industrial auxiliary processes are the most technically backward activity of the entire Soviet economy. And backwardness in this sector ties up scarce manpower, impeding the full effect on labor productivity of new production equipment and processes.

As with the modernization goals, however, success in machanizing auxiliary processes depends largely on the ability of domestic machine builders to turn out large quantities of materials-handling equipment which often must be tailored to very specific uses. While production of equipment for mechanization of auxiliary processes is scheduled to double during 1976-80 compared with 1971-75, complaints are already being heard that many types of small-scale mechanization are not included in the plan, and resources for their production are not being provided. Thus, the supply of general-purpose equipment for mechanization likely will provide only a marginal boost to labor productivity since production is

18

largely unspecialized and the necessary volume is not likely to become available.(8)

CONSTRAINTS ON CAPITAL FORMATION

Redirecting the emphasis of the USSR's capital formation policy will not be easy. A variety of exogenous factors makes accomplishment more difficult, but at the same time, all the more imperative.

Continued industrial expansion in Siberia requires large outlays for new productive plant and overhead facilities. The necessity to utilize less rich ore deposits requires construction of more extensive (and more costly) processing facilities. The higher proportion of industrial investment in raw materials, as distinguished from manufacturing sectors, involves a heavier construction component. The belated decisions to invest in projects which would alleviate environmental disruption also imply proportionately higher construction outlays.(9)

Finally, the heavy burden placed on domestic machine building by the programs of modernization and mechanization will require substantial qualitative and quantitative improvements in the raw materials and semi-finished products supplied to the machinery sector by other branches of industry, especially the ferrous metals and energy producing branches. The necessary improvements, however, will be particularly hard to achieve in part because many qualitative improvements can be realized only after modernization of plant and equipment has occurred, and, in part, because quantitative increases are becoming more and more costly to maintain.

Rising Costs

Capital costs, especially in extractive industries, are rising more rapidly than output primarily due to the declining quality of readily available raw materials. In ferrous

----

(8)

The Soviets see increased use of numerically controlled (NC) machine tools as one answer to higher productivity. However, a quantum improvement in the quality and capabilities of Soviet NC machines will be needed, as well as a greater willingness by industry to use them, before their potential effectiveness can be realized.

(9)

Cohn, op. cit., p. 459.

metallurgy, for example, capital costs are being driven up in the mining sector because of the declining quality of ore and the need for increased beneficiation. Similarly, in petroleum extraction the cost of purchasing specialized equipment to cope with deep drilling requirements and water encroachment is forcing the USSR to spend more for each barrel of oil produced. In the electric power industry, capital costs are rising as construction of thermal power plants declines in favor of nuclear and hydroelectric facilities.

Increasing Dependence on Siberia

Continued economic growth of the USSR and of its allies in Eastern Europe is becoming increasingly dependent on the exploitation of Siberian resources, particularly with respect to energy. Developing new sources of energy and other raw materials in the East, however, will require heavy capital investment -- much of which will consist of construction activity. And construction costs in the eastern regions range from 30 percent higher to more than double those in the European part of the country. Moreover, most of the areas where resources must be developed will require not only the basic facilities for exploration and exploitation but also the associated infrastructure, e.g., roads, housing, cultural, and service facilities if permanent industrial centers are to flourish. Thus, the need to accelerate industrial development in the eastern regions will absorb, to some extent, the intended gains from cutting back on new construction starts and could reult in increasing the share of construction in total investment, given the low rate of growth planned for investment through 1980. On the other hand, if new construction starts in the east are not forthcoming -- particularly for fuels and power -- the Soviet economy could suffer a shortage of essential materials in the 1980s.(10)

----

(10)
This concern was expressed by the minister of the coal industry at the 25th Party Congress. "The CPSU Central Committee draft for the 25th Congress outlines the development of the Kansk-Achinsk basin. But the 5-year plan does not provide for resources for starting the construction of new projects. We ask the USSR Gosplan to allocate the necessary material and financial means, when it amends the 1976-80 plan, bearing in mind that it will take 10-15 years to create enterprises in new, sparsely inhabited areas."

Imbalances in New Capacity

To a large extent, both the quality and quantity of key industrial materials -- notably steel and electric power -- obtained over the next few years depend on the amount and type of new capacity brought on stream. This, in turn, hinges on maintaining a careful balance between completing projects now under construction and starting new construction projects. An all out Soviet style compaign to concentrate on project completions at the expense of new starts could result in serious imbalances in the availability of new production capacity. For example, a plant completed now might depend on materials inputs from plants whose construction has been postponed.

Equally important to increasing new capacity is the performance of the machinery sector. In the past, increases in new capacity in nearly all sectors have been retarded by problems in the supply of machinery and equipment. While some improvement can be expected if the structure of investment shifts markedly from construction to machinery, it is likely that shortfalls in new capacity will continue to plague the industrial materials sectors, particularly electric power where most new capacity is to occur in nuclear and hydroelectric powerplants. Even if new power capacity is installed on schedule, electric power will remain in tight supply in the western USSR -- where 80% of electricity is consumed -- until high voltage direct current transmission technology has been mastered; probably not before the mid-1980's. Thus the output of electric power produced between now and 1980 may prove insufficient to supply fully the program of industrial modernization and at the same time supply large increases of electricity to the population. If shortages occur, industry would probably bear the burden of any reduced growth in electric power production.(11)

The domestic production of high quality steel and steel products will also be influenced by the acquisition (or lack thereof) of new capacity. Much of the existing capacity for rolled sheet steel is very old and technically obsolete. New and improved mills are being installed but far too slowly to keep pace with growing needs. Major deficiencies exist with respect to equipment for the production of cold rolled sheet, high quality transformer sheet, tinplate, and other coated steel, and large diameter pipe. Substantial investment has

----

(11)
During 1971-75 the industrial sector suffered 77% of the shortfall in planned power consumption.

21

been concentrated in basic production sectors -- pig iron and ore mining(12) -- at the expense of facilities to improve the quality and assortment of steel products. As a result, the USSR has had to rely increasingly on imports to meet its domestic requirements for finished steel.(13)

Comparison of long-term trends in Soviet production and consumption of finished rolled steel suggests that production through 1980 will continue to fall short of needs and that the USSR's dependence on imported steel will increase. The USSR also will rely more heavily on foreign sources for metallurgical equipment to expand and modernize the domestic facilities for production of finished rolled steel products. In addition, Soviet needs for imported steel will continue into the 1980s, as programs for development of the eastern regions gain importance and as modernization and expansion of facilities in established steelmaking centers continue.

Reliance on Foreign Technology

The acquisition of advanced foreign technology is one of the cornerstones of the current Soviet growth strategy, although the leadership probably overestimates the overall impact of such technology. Soviet imports of Western plant and machinery through 1980 will not provide a dramatic boost to either the capital formation program or the industrial growth rate. Even if machinery imports are maintained at $5-$6 billion a year during 1976-80, and all are directed to industry, the share of foreign machinery in the stock of Soviet industrial machinery and equipment will still be small. However, imported machinery may be crucial to continued rapid growth in selected industries, such as chemicals.

The major effect of imported machinery is that it permits the USSR to put new capacity into production despite bottlenecks in its own machinery industry and frees domestic resources for other investment and production programs. Imports of Western technology also may help to ease some bottlenecks now threatening future growth. For example, heavy earthmoving equipment, petroleum and mining equipment, and technology for Siberian development are essential for

----

(12)
    The share of fixed capital in ferrous metallurgy absorbed
    by mining and processing of ores increased from 12% in
    1960 to 21% in 1972.
(13)
    Imports of finished steel increased from 8 million tons
    during 1966-70 to about 27 million tons in 1971-75.

maintaining an adequate and timely flow of raw materials to industry. Large-scale acquisition of Western computer and semiconductor technology could also break supply bottlenecks in those key industries. The effects of modern high capacity data processing equipment would be felt throughout the economy, both in the civilian and military sectors. Access to a reliable domestic supply of advanced Western-type semiconductors could speed Soviet commercialization of large computers and complex electronic systems and instrumentation for advanced weapons.

However, pressure for large increases in imports of Western technology and equipment to counter bottlenecks will likely continue, and may become more acute, in the 1980's -- particularly as the USSR strives to locate and exploit new oil and gas resources to counter the output effects of depletion of the deposits now under exploitation. Continued increases of imported equipment will be contingent upon Moscow's hard currency debt position which is likely to worsen considerably in the next few years.

Perhaps more important, importation of Western technology could prove unsatisfactory as a basic tenet of Soviet growth strategy if the domestic economy remains no more capable than in the past of generating its own technical progress. First, the industrial sector is so large that the overall impact of imported technology must be modest. The overwhelming proportion of the nation's annual increments in capital equipment will have to come from domestic production. Hence, unless the general level of domestic technology improves, the contribution of technological progress to overall growth is likely to remain small. Second, the technology of advanced Western countries may fail to mesh well with existing Soviet equipment, available labor skills, and methods of operation.(14) Unless the general level of technological and managerial skills in the USSR rises substantially, imported equipment is likely to operate at lower levels of productivity than intended by the exporting country, or expected by the Soviets, thus losing some of the gains from trade.

Third, and most important, the USSR cannot expect to project itself into the ranks of the leaders in the generation of new technology by relying on imports for its most advanced technology. The lead times for the most advanced and rapidly

----

(14)
    In the case of the Kama truck factory, Western engineers estimate that several years will be required to integrate all of the imported equipment into smooth operation.

23

changing technology are such that by the time equipment is imported, it will already have begun to obsolesce. Imported technology, therefore cannot serve as a substitute for a technologically innovative economic system. While some gains will occur from imports, they will be mostly superficial and temporary. Soviet engineers will note well what foreign designers have done -- but, not having gone through the designing experience, will be ill prepared to carry the design to a still more advanced level.(15)

EFFICIENCY OF RESOURCE USE

The drive to acquire high technology equipment reflects an attempt to offset through rapid technological advances diminishing returns to investment that have slowed Soviet growth. Because the principal carrier of new technology into the production process is new machinery and equipment, the leadership hopes that by shifting investment from construction activity to machinery and equipment, they will be able to rely more heavily on productivity gains as the major source of growth -- particularly in industry. For the reasons outlined above, however, the effectiveness of this investment strategy will fall far short of expectations, and the anticipated acceleration in the productivity of labor and capital inputs probably will not materialize (see Table 2.1).

In the past, shortfalls in attaining productivity goals were partly offset by overfulfillment of industrial employment plans. However, this reserve is much smaller than in the past and will become smaller yet after 1980. The growth of the working-age population then will be less than one-half percent annually compared with an average of 1.7% in the 1970s.(16) Compounding the effects of this slowdown in the labor force is the fact that most of the increase from now through the 1980s will occur among the non-Slavic (principally Turkic) minorities who have yet to migrate in significant numbers from Central Asia to labor-short industrial areas in European and Siberian parts of the country.

Neither past trends in productivity growth nor the present outlook for technological gains, management reform,

----

(15) For a detailed treatment of the Soviet experience with technological innovation, see Joseph S. Berliner, The Innovation Decision in Soviet Industry, 1976.
(16)
This issue is discussed in Philip Grossman's paper in this volume.

24

TABLE 2.1
USSR: Inputs, Output and Factor Productivity in Industry
(Average Annual Rates of Growth in Percentages)

	1961-65	1966-70	1971-75	1976-77	Plan 1976-80
Total inputs(a)	6.8	5.7	4.8	N.A.(c)	3.7
Man-hours worked	2.9	3.1	1.5	2.2	0.7
Capital	11.2	8.7	8.7	N.A.	7.0
Output	6.5	6.3	6.0	3.9	6.3
Factor productivity(b)	-0.3	0.6	1.1	N.A.	2.5

a. Inputs of man-hours and capital are combined using weights
    of 52.4 percent and 47.6 percent, respectively, in a
    Cobb-Douglas (linear homogenous)   production function.
    These weights represent the distribution of labor costs
    (wages and social insurance deductions) and capital costs
    (depreciation and a 20 percent charge on gross fixed
    capital) in 1970, the base year for all indexes underlying
    the growth rate calculations.
b. The growth of combined factor productivity represents the
    growth in output per combined unit of labor and capital
    services.
c. Not available.

and improved worker incentives appear to support the exceptionally high rate of growth of productivity in industry implied in the Tenth Five Year Plan. Although the growth of industrial factor productivity may accelerate somewhat, it is unlikely to exceed an average annual rate of 1 to 1.5%. Since the limits to increasing industrial employment are more stringent now than in the past, efforts to augment the industrial labor force probably will not result in a growth of manhours of labor higher than about 1% per year. Such rates of increase in factor productivity and man-hours, together with the planned growth of industrial gross fixed capital stock would yield a range of industrial growth from 4.9% to 5.4% per year. Even this projection may be optimistic, given the exceptionally poor performance in 1976 and 1977.

The growth in industrial output during the last two years has declined sharply from previous rates (see Table 2.2). The drop has been felt most severely in the production of material inputs -- notably fuels, power, and steel. Among the numerous ills of Soviet industry, problems in producing steel are currently the most serious. Because of the difficulties in this basic area, even the growth of machinery -- usually a star performer -- has slowed substantially. Partly because of the poor fit between demand and supply of steel products, rolled and tubular steel output slowed to a two percent growth in 1976 and virtually stagnated in 1977.

The recent performance in the area of capital formation has been particularly disappointing to the leadership. Despite efforts to concentrate investment on modernization of existing assets and completion of projects already begun, the growth of new plant and equipment fell to an all time low in 1976 and 1977, and the backlog of unfinished projects increased sharply because of slow procurement and installation of equipment (see Table 2.3). Continued inability to bring new capacity on-stream more rapidly, together with new construction starts foregone, will lead to a marked slowdown in capital formation by the mid 1980s. This will depress the growth of output even further -- particularly if no gains are made in raising the productivity of capital. Here, the Soviet record is not encouraging. Much of the new plant and equipment being incorporated into the stock of capital is technologically similar to that already in existence. In addition, barriers to innovation and substitution of capital for labor are formidable. Enterprise managers resist introducing new processes or equipment because it disrupts production processes in the short run; they also continue to hoard workers as a safety factor to ensure plan fulfillment. Moreover, inordinate delays in planning, design, and construction of new production facilities encourage retention of obsolescent plant and equipment in order to meet the

TABLE 2.2
USSR: Recent Industrial Performance (Average Annual Rates of Growth in Percentages)

	1971-75	1976	1977
Materials	5.4	3.8	2.8
Electric power	7.0	6.9	3.5
Fuels	5.0	4.8	4.0
Ferrous metals	3.9	2.8	0.8
Nonferrous metals	6.0	2.0	2.0
Woodworking and paper	2.5	1.3	1.2
Construction materials	5.2	2.4	1.2
Chemicals	8.5	5.0	5.4
Machinery	8.3	6.4	6.0
Consumer nondurables	3.5	-0.4	3.5
Soft goods	2.6	3.6	1.8
Processed food	4.3	-3.9	5.1
Total industry	6.0	3.8	4.1

Source: Data were derived from updated version of growth indexes presented by Rush V. Greenslade, The Real Gross National Product of the USSR, 1950-1975 in JEC compendium Soviet Economy in a New Perspective, October 1976, pp. 269-300.

TABLE 2.3
USSR: Indicators of Total Capital Formation
(Average Annual Rates of Growth in Percentages)

	1971-75	1976	Preliminary 1977
Gross new fixed investment	7.0	4.5	2.9
Gross additions of new fixed capital	6.7	1.4	2.7
Unfinished construction	7.9	9.6	10.7
Capital stock (end year)	7.9	7.2	6.3
Retirement rate	1.4	1.3	1.9

Source: Derived from data in Narkhoz 1976, pp. 80-81, 423,
432, and 447.   Data for 1977 estimated from Garbuzov and
Baibakov speeches, December 1977 and plan fulfillment report
in Pravda, 28 January 1978.

overriding priority of achieving the output plan. The effect of such rigidities is a pervasive tendency of the system to reproduce itself in the same mix of output and the same pattern of investment.

Increasing the rate of investment much beyond the currently planned rate between now and the mid-1980s will not be a viable alternative if defense spending continues at its current pace and some growth in per-capita consumption is assumed.

If growth in both defense and investment were to be maintained at annual rate of 4 to 5% over the next eight years, growth in per capita consumption probably would fall below 2% per year. On the other hand, to keep the growth of per-capita consumption between 3 to 4% per year and boost investment growth to 4 to 5% per year, defense spending probably could not grow by more than 1 to 2% per year.

Any attempt to boost consumption through the output effects of increased investment would be ineffective except in the very long run. First, increases in the growth rate of investment have marginal effects on the already large capital stock and therefore on output. Second, the return on new capital is lower than in the past due to the expected slowdown in labor force growth. Third, the leadership's program to raise the return on investment, as already discussed, is fraught with difficulty.

During the past year, energy production also has experienced declining rates of growth. Indeed, the increase in electric power fell to an unprecedented low in 1977. Oil and gas production also slowed and more incidents of fuel shortages were reported in the Soviet press. As a result Moscow has recently stepped up efforts to encourage conservation at all levels.

The more difficult issue of long-term restructuring of the economy for energy saving also is being discussed in the Soviet press. Here, special attention is being directed to the introduction of less energy-intensive machines and processes.

Technically the Soviets can achieve energy savings in three ways:

- First, by stricter allocation measures designed to encourage or even force conservation.

- Second, by retooling and installing machinery and equipment that uses less energy per unit of output.

29

- And third, by adjusting the mix of production away from energy-intensive activity such as construction and investment goods, and toward less energy-intensive activity like light industry products and services.

Looking more closely at these issues, one notes that the limited flexibility in the Soviet economic system forces the leadership to tighten the administrative screws gradually on energy availability lest more stringent allocation measures disrupt deliveries to industrial customers and multiply supply bottlenecks throughout the economy.

Retooling and installing more energy-efficient equipment promises significant savings -- but only in the long run and after considerable expense. Enterprise managers will be reluctant to scrap equipment that has served them well -- in fulfilling past plans and earning bonuses -- in order to install potentially energy-efficient equipment of unknown reliability. Finally, a massive capital production and installation program would itself consume significant quantities of fuel.

Shifting from the production of energy-intensive goods to goods and services that can be produced with less energy would challenge the long-established priority of heavy industry. Because the most energy-intensive sectors are construction and investment goods, reduction in the growth of their output would cut into future production and reduce the long-term growth rate of the economy as a whole.

Changing the mix of output would have ramifications throughout the economy. Production and inter-industry deliveries would have to be changed and rebalanced to reflect the new mix of goods and services coming out of the economic system.

For the moment, the Soviet leadership appears to be avoiding hard decisions and bold solutions. Whichever way the leadership goes, it seems certain the the inflexibility of the Soviet economic system -- fostered by years of rigid resource allocation and a built-in aversion to innovation -- will make it difficult, if not impossible to achieve significant results quickly, certainly not quickly enough to cope effectively with the growing pressure on current energy production -- particularly oil.

30

CONCLUSION

In view of the lackluster performance of the past two years, as well as problematic future supplies of labor and capital and likely gains in productivity, we feel that Soviet GNP will grow in the neighborhood of 4% annually during the remainder of the seventies. Achievement of even a 4% increase in GNP will depend heavily upon the Soviets' ability to:

- break the bottleneck in steel output;

- reduce sharply the growing backlog of unfinished construction and uninstalled equipment;

- obtain unexpectedly large increases of oil from West Siberia; and

- achieve major efficiencies in the use of material resources, especially energy and ferrous metals.

As always, a critical element in Soviet economic performance in the short term is agriculture. The growth of GNP over the rest of this decade could fall substantially from the expected average rate of about 4%, if -- as is likely -- weather fluctuations reduce harvests.

Beyond 1980 the pace of economic growth is likely to slow further as the pinch on human and natural resources tightens. No programs are now in-train or even on the horizon that presage a quantum leap in factor productivity. In the absence of any dramatic departures from past policies, the growth of GNP in 1981-85 can therefore be expected to decline to around 3 to 3.5% annually. Clearly the Soviets will have to rely on imports for some key equipment and semi-finished products. The capital formation strategy, however -- particularly the modernization program -- may be squeezed between hard currency deficits on one side and the need to sustain growth in domestic production and increase development in the Eastern regions of the country on the other.

31

3

THE SOVIET UNION AND THE WORLD ECONOMY IN THE 1980S: A REVIEW OF THE ALTERNATIVES

Donald W. Green
Chase Manhattan Bank, N.A.

INTRODUCTION

The objective of this chapter is to sketch the likely development of Soviet economic relations with the World Economy over the decade 1976-1985, the period of the Tenth and Eleventh Five-Year plans. In preparing this analysis we have utilized SOVMOD III, the third-generation econometric model developed jointly by SRI International and Wharton Econometric Forecasting Associates.(2) In the first section of this paper, we shall review the major linkages between the Soviet and World Economies and the representation of those linkages

----

(1)

The views expressed are the responsibility of the author alone and do not necessarily reflect those of Chase Manhattan Bank. I wish to acknowledge the contributions of Daniel Bond and Peter Miovic in the preparation of the SOVMOD III projections used in this paper without, of course, holding them responsible for the conclusions drawn.

(2)

A full discussion of model structure and properties for the Soviet Econometric Model appears in Donald W. Green and Christopher I. Higgins, SOVMOD I: A Macroeconometric Model of the Soviet Union (New York: Academic Press, 1977). An earlier version of SOVMOD III is described and documented in Donald W. Green, Gene D. Guill, Lawrence R. Klein, Herbert S. Levine, Peter Miovic, and Ross S. Preston, The SRI-WEFA Soviet Econometric Model: Phase Three Documentation, Volumes I and II, SRI International, SSC-TN-2970-5&6, May 1977.

within the specification of the model. Then the foreign trade implications of a Baseline Solution for the period 1976-1985 will be examined in detail, with the Solution included as Appendix A to this chapter. Two alternative outcomes are then constructed and compared with the Baseline Solution: (1) a more restrictive world economy and less favorable weather conditions in the USSR; and (2) stagnation in Soviet oil production in the 1980s. A final section will summarize the implications of those alternative paths for the USSR's role in the World Economy of the 1980s.

A REVIEW OF THE MAJOR LINKS BETWEEN
THE SOVIET ECONOMY AND THE REST OF THE WORLD

For many years, Western and Soviet economists often stressed the "autarky" of centrally-planned economies and the limited role played by foreign trade in the industrialization of the Soviet Union. Actually, Western technology played an important role in Soviet development during the First Five-Year Plan (1928-1932), a role which has been neglected until recently.(3) Certainly since the mid-1960s, there has been a growing relationship between the Soviet and World economies. Soviet growth prospects can no longer be considered in isolation apart from the conditions in world markets for energy, raw materials, agricultural goods, technology, and credit.(4)

While it is generally not true that "everything depends upon everything else," the complexity of technology and behavior in modern industrial economies forces the economist

----

(3)

> For a documentation of this role of Western technology, see Anthony C. Sutton, Western Technology and Soviet Economic Development, 1917 to 1930, Vol. 1 (Stanford, Cal.: Hoover Institution Press, 1968). An evaluation of Soviet decision-making and Western policy during this period is provided in Michael R. Dohan, "The Economic Origins of Soviet Autarky 1927/28-1934," Slavic Review, 35 (December 1976), 603-635.

(4)

> More comprehensive studies of the Soviet foreign trade system and the expension of East-West trade are provided in Marshall I. Goldman, Detente and Dollars: Doing Business with the Soviet Union (New York: Basic Books, 1975); Franklyn D. Holzman, International Trade Under Communism-Politics and Economics (New York: Basic Books, 1976).

to focus on key relationships in his analysis. In this section we shall attempt to simplify our task by focusing upon three major links between the Soviet economy and the rest of the world:

- the fuel and materials link;

- the technology transfer and credit link; and

- the agricultural commodity link.

In the discussion of each link, the structure of the interdependence will be briefly sketched on the basis of available analysis. Particular attention will be given to the representation of that link in the specification of SOVMOD III.(5) This will assist the reader in appraising quantitative relations which underlie the projections described in later sections of the chapter.

The foreign trade sector of SOVMOD III distinguishes Soviet trade with four geographical areas: the Council of Mutual Economic Assistance (CMEA), the Developed West (including Japan, Australia and New Zealand), Other Socialist Countries (Yugoslavia, China, Cuba, North Korea, Vietnam), and the Less Developed Countries (LDCs). In this review we will emphasize Soviet trade with the CMEA and the West, accounting for over three-quarters of the value of Soviet foreign trade. Soviet trade with the Middle East and the larger developing countries (Brazil, India, Mexico) will become increasingly important over the next decade, but the available quantitative record is too weak to support long term projections for those areas. In aggregate terms, Soviet trade with individual LDCs and other Socialist Economies has been quite erratic because of political influences, but the longer trends have been systematically related to Soviet agricultural performance and to import volume among LDCs.

Trade between the Soviet Union and Eastern Europe (the CMEA Six: Bulgaria, Czechoslovakia, German Democratic Republic, Hungary, Poland, and Romania) has been disaggregated into four commodity groups: machinery, raw materials, food, other consumer goods. In general these trade flows are related to activity levels in the respective areas (industry,

----

(5)
    We shall not examine the technical issues of specification and estimation in this paper. The foreign trade equations of SOVMOD III will be evaluated in detail in forthcoming studies.

34

agriculture, investment, consumption, etc.) and bilateral adjustment processes which introduce a minor role for intra-CMEA prices. Soviet trade with the West has been similarly disaggregated in commodity groups with an additional distinction between fuel and other materials for Soviet exports. Soviet exports to the West depend upon activity in Western economies, world trade prices, and the level of indebtedness. Soviet imports from the West depend upon levels of activity in the Soviet economy and are constrained by the relationship betwen debt service and exports. An important sector of SOVMOD III determines hard currency liquidity, defined as the deviation of the actual debt service ratio from a target ratio. The debt service ratio measures the repayment of medium-term and long term debt plus interest as a percentage of Soviet exports to the West. The impact of detente on Soviet behavior has now been introduced through an upward shift in the debt service ratio target from the late 1960s through 1980. The balancing item in the Soviet hard currency accounts is the level of net foreign exchange reserves (foreign exchange held in Western banks less short term debt). The change in net reserves is a function of the balance of trade in convertible currencies, debt repayment, interest payments, the net balance of services and transfers, credit drawings in the West, and gold sales.

Fuel and Materials

This link between the Soviet and World economies has received growing attention because of Western concern with the future prospects of Soviet oil production and the consequences for the world energy balance. The major determinants of the Soviet balance of fuel and other materials are indicated in Figure 3.1. Soviet production of basic materials (coal, petroleum, natural gas, ferrous and nonferrous ores and metals, lumber, etc.) is primarily a function of fixed capital in those branches and there are usually long gestation periods for large projects. Domestic consumption of those materials is determined by aggregate industrial output with some longrun change due to compositional shifts within industry.

Foreign trade flows of materials can then be related to net Soviet output. In the past, Soviet exports of fuel and materials to the CMEA were a function of net material product in Eastern Europe and also determined a smaller flow of material imports from the CMEA. Material imports from the West are determined by Soviet industrial activity subject to a liquidity constraint for hard currency. Exports of fuel and materials to the West are determined by Western industrial activity, world materials prices, and the level of Soviet debt.

Figure 3.1

THE FUEL AND MATERIALS LINK

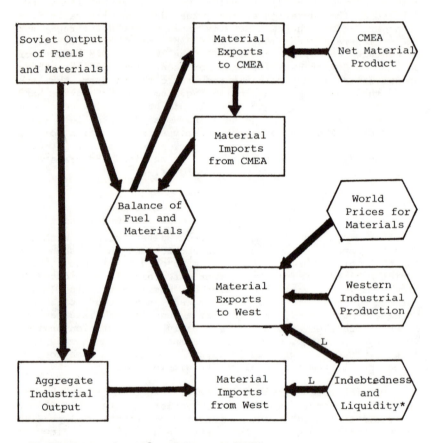

L indicates a lag of one year or more.
*See Figure 3.2 for the determination of indebtedness and
liquidity

Many features of this link are present in SOVMOD III but certain aspects have not been modelled. The explicit treatment of the Soviet balance of materials using the input-output system of SOVMOD III remains a task for current research and the intra-CMEA flows of raw materials have not been related to Soviet net production. Consequently, the analyst must adjust those trade flows within the model solution if those responses are judged important. Soviet exports of fuel to the West have been related to a proxy for the net domestic fuel balance (the difference between the growth rate of total industry and the growth rate for petroleum and gas), but the magnitude of the estimated response, based on past experience, now appears to be too small. In the energy scenario discussed in Section 3, exports of fuel to both the CMEA aned the West will be adjusted on the basis of analyst judgment. However, the market demand parameters and the Soviet response parameters (to debt and liquidity) in the estimated equations are used in those projections.

Technology Transfer and Western Credit

During the construction of the Soviet Econometric Model a new methodology was developed for evaluating the quantitative impact of imported machinery on Soviet industrial production; to a certain extent, this technique provides a measure of the gains from technology transfer. The incorporation of this feature within the complete macroeconometric model provides a framework for evaluating the direct and indirect benefits of Soviet machinery imports.(6) New capital investment is determined by the Plan for centralized capital investment, defense expenditures, gross profits, and the stage of the Five-Year Plan. Capital formation depends upon current and past investment expenditures and the stage of the Five-Year Plan. Industrial output is a function of employment, capital,

----

(6)
    The rise of machinery imports as a proxy for technology transfer has been presented and evaluated in two earlier p apers: Donald W. Green and Herbert S. Levine, "Implications of Technology Transfers for the USSR," in NATO, Economic Directorate, East-West Technological Cooperation (Brussels: NATO, 1976); and Donald W. Green and Herbert S. Levine, "Macroeconomic Evidence of the Value of Machinery Imports to the Soviet Union," in J.R. Thomas and U. M. Kruse-Vaucienne, Soviet Science and Technology: Domestic and Foreign Perspectives (Washington, D.C.,: George Washington University, 1977).

and a stock measure of foreign capital where the specification is a Cobb-Douglas production function.

Demand functions for imported machinery in open capitalist economies usually include a more aggregate category of demand (e.g., total demand for machinery and equipment) and a relative price term indicating the competitiveness of domestic machinery in the world market. Decision agents are, by hypothesis, profit-maximizing enterprises and not national governments. The specification of Soviet demand functions for foreign machinery, however, must take into account the existence of the foreign trade monopoly and the disequilibrium price set for foreign exchange. Foreign exchange, particularly hard currency, is a scarce resource rationed by the Ministry of Foreign Trade under the direction of the Council of Ministers and Gosplan. Ministries and enterprises compete, through both political and economic channels, for imported machinery as for other scarce economic resources.

As in other components of the Soviet macromodel, we have sought to specify the pattern of bureaucratic regularity (rules of thumb), identify contingencies to which such bureaucratic rules must respond, and clarify where possible the role of administrative intervention in shifting the rule. The "rule of thumb" in our specification is that the real level of machinery purchased abroad moves proportionately with the total level of capital investment within a given sector. The ratio, however, adjusts to conditions of hard currency liquidity, i.e., it will rise if the debt service target is raised, or fall if the actual debt service ratio rises.

This structure is presented in Figure 3.2 along with an elaboration of the determinants of Soviet indebtedness and hard currency liquidity. An increase in world material prices or Western industrial activity will boost the value of Soviet exports. This boost in exports will lower the debt service ratio, and with an unchanged target, will boost machinery imports and subsequent industrial production. This process tends to limit itself eventually because of two feedback loops. First, export growth is restrained after a lag because of reduced indebtedness. Second, the rise in Soviet imports will eventually raise indebtedness again and therefore reduce Soviet liquidity.

Most of this technology transfer and credit link has been incorporated within SOVMOD III. The productive impact of imported machinery has only been identified for the important branches of petroleum and gas, machine-building and metal-working, and chemicals and petrochemicals. However, aggregate import demand functions make the hard currency implications of technology transfer more general. The

38

Figure 3.2

THE TECHNOLOGY TRANSFER AND CREDIT LINK

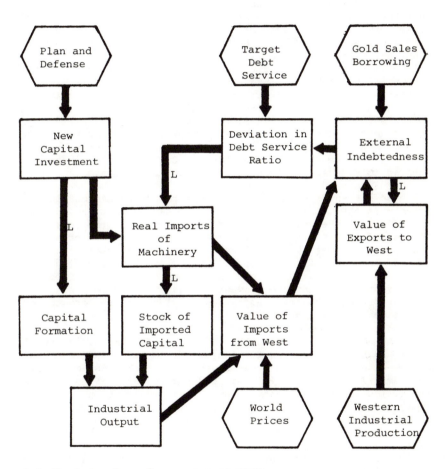

L indicates a lag of one year or more

behavioral system has remained partly discretionary in the model, with gold sales, credit drawings, and the target debt service ratio being exogenous variables set by the analyst. The measure of debt service used in the model relates only to medium and long term debt, so the dynamics of the indebtedness system under scenarios depends upon the assumptions made concerning Soviet credit drawings.

Agricultural Commodities

The agricultural sector of SOVMOD III has been recently extended and refined to evaluate the interdependencies between crop production, animal production and the growth in the livestock herd. The link between Soviet agricultural output and agricultural trade with the CMEA and the West is diagrammed in Figure 3.3. The scale of Soviet agricultural trade flows is determined by "normal" Soviet agricultural output, and shortrun variation is dependent upon the deviation of the actual harvest from normal output.(7) Agricultural exports to the CMEA (primarily grain) depend upon past Soviet grain harvest conditions. Soviet agricultural imports from the CMEA are scaled by Soviet food consumption and vary with CMEA and Soviet harvest conditions. CMEA food prices do not appear to have any behavioral impact on real flows.

Soviet exports of grain to Western Europe and developing countries virtually ended in 1972. Other Soviet food exports depend upon the previous year's harvest and the level of Western food prices. Soviet real agricultural imports from the West (primarily grain) depend on the current and past grain harvests with the world grain price influencing the value of expenditures but not the volume of imports. Feed fed to livestock depends upon domestic grain production and grain imports, and the level of feed influences the growth of livestock with a lag.

A major problem with the modelling of this agricultural link has been the demonstration of an impact of agricultural trade on consumption and feed fed to livestock. While certain econometric results have appeared promising, refinement in specification and estimation during the construction of SOVMOD

----

(7)
The definitions of "normal" output and the harvest deviation are given in a forthcoming paper along with a full description of the agricultural sector of SOVMOD III; Donald W. Green, "An Econometric Model of Soviet Agriculture," SRI-WEFA Project Working paper #58, September 1977.

Figure 3.3

THE AGRICULTURAL COMMODITY LINK

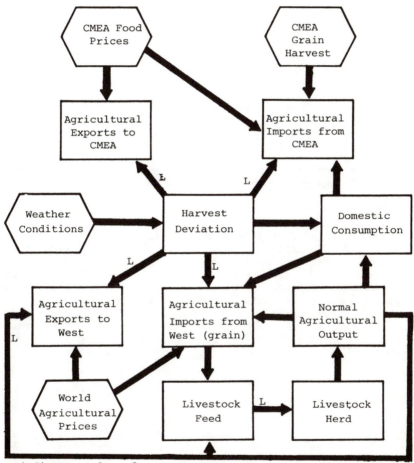

L indicates a lag of one year or more

41

III did not indicate statistical significance for those hypotheses. Furthermore, the grain import variable has been exogenized for most projections given the U.S.-U.S.S.R. grain agreement for 1977-1981. The impact of Soviet agricultural performance on trade flows is represented in the model so that hard currency expenditures on grain will tend to restrain other imports and boost Soviet exports.

A BASELINE SOLUTION TO 1985: THE GROWTH AND COMPOSITION OF SOVIET FOREIGN TRADE IN A BUOYANT WORLD ECONOMY(8)

A baseline solution obtained with an econometric model implies a judgment of plausibility and internal consistency by the analyst. It does not necessarily represent the most likely path of the economy nor the desirable path according to any criterion. The major elements which determine such a baseline solution are:

- the model itself;

- the assumptions made concerning the external environment and strategic policy decisions; and

- modifications and adjustments introduced by the analyst.

The Model

The projections presented in this paper were computed using a 1977 version of SOVMOD III, the third generation SRI-WEFA Soviet Econometric Model, whose foreign trade sector was described in the preceding section. The first long-run projections with SOVMOD began as early as 1974, and the current baseline solution has evolved through several stages of model development, benefitting from the criticisms and suggestions of many scholars. The current SOVMOD III has been estimated through 1975; it consequently projects historical experience from the 1958-1975 period forward through 1985.

----

(8) This Baseline Solution to 1985 is discussed in greater detail in a forthcoming publication: Donald W. Green and Herbert S. Levine, The Soviet Economy in the 1980s, McGraw-Hill, 1978. In this chapter, the domestic consequences of scenarios are discussed only briefly with our major concern being Soviet foreign trade.

The Assumptions

In the preparation of this Baseline Projection, we have concentrated on the information provided by the econometric model given our assumptions concerning the external environment and the strategic policy decisions by Soviet leaders. Among the environmental assumptions, the most important concern demographic trends, weather conditions and the world economy:

Demographic Assumptions. The total population of the USSR and the population of able-bodied ages were projected on the basis of the estimates prepared by the Foreign Demographic Analysis Division of the U.S. Department of Commerce.(9) These projections indicate an annual rate of growth of the able-bodied population of 1.5% in the period 1976-1980 with that rate falling to 0.4% during the 1980's. The economic impact of this decline in the growth of the potential labor force will be accentuated by its geographic pattern. The growth will be heavily concentrated during the 1980's in Central Asia, Kazakhstan, and the Transcaucasian Region. The working-age population is actually projected to decline in the Russian SFSR during the 1980's, while remaining virtually unchanged in the Ukraine and Baltic region.(10)

Weather Conditions. The role of weather conditions is included in the model through variables for precipitation and temperature. These indices are measured as deviations from "normal" conditions, where "normal" is defined as the period 1960-1973. For the projection period these variables are set equal to zero, thus representing an assumption of steady "normal" weather conditions. Since there is a widely-held scientific opinion that the 1960-1973 period was above normal in the longer term, the first scenario presented in Section 3 will examine the potential impact of less favorable weather on Soviet growth prospects.

----

(9)
Stephen Rapawy, Estimates and Projections of the Labor Force and Civilian Employment in the USSR 1950-1990 U.S. Department of Commerce, Bureau of Economic Analysis, September 1976.

(10)
See Chapter 6 in the present volume, and Murray Feshbach and Stephen Rapawy, "Soviet Population and Manpower Trends and Policies", in U.S. Congress, Soviet Economy in a New Perspective (Washington, 1976)

43

The World Economy. In the Baseline solution, we have generally accepted a projection of buoyant world economic conditions, assumptions which were adopted in the early 1977 projections of the Wharton Annual and Industry Model of the United States. After the pause of 1977, industrial projection in the West is projected to grow at approximately 5% per year with total imports growing 7% per year to 1980 and at slightly less than 6% in the 1980's. Developed West imports of fuel and materials are projected to grow at 7% per year though 1985. Among the developing countries, annual growth of total imports is projected at 7% for the period 1977-1985. Following the revised five-year plans of the Council for Mutual Economic Assistance (CMEA), CMEA net material product is projected to grow 6.5% per year through 1980 and at 6% during the 1980's.

In the foreign trade equations of SOVMOD, selected prices have been used as deflators and for the estimation of price elasticities. Generally, we have assumed conditions of moderate inflation in the world market with slightly less inflation in CMEA trade. The Soviet Union is expected to experience a modest gain in its terms of trade, with official import prices rising 4% and export prices rising 5% per year. Raw material and fuel prices are projected to rise 7% annually in the world market with machinery prices rising slightly less at 6%. CMEA fuel prices are projected to rise more rapidly than prices for other raw materials, with the differential rising by 15% over the decade 1976-1985. After 1977, world prices for grain and gold are projected to rise at 2% and 3% per year, respectively.

In using the Soviet model, the analyst must also introduce strategic assumptions which reflect internal political decisions. The most important of these strategic variables relate to defense expenditures, the rate of capital accumulation, and the management of the hard currency balance.

Soviet Defense Expenditures. In the Baseline Solution, the level of military manpower is projected to remain constant at four million men. Defense non-personnel expenditures plus outlays for State reserves (the SOVMOD measure of military procurement) have been assumed to grow 4% per year. Military R&D expenditures are also projected to grow 4% annually through 1985. These assumptions for Soviet defense expenditures result in a stable defense share in GNP over the projection period.

The Planned Rate of Capital Accumulation. Following the indicators of the 10th FYP, the planned annual growth rate for centralized investment in new fixed capital is projected at 4%

44

through 1985; this represents a substantial reduction from the 7.5% mean growth rate during 1960-1975. The financing targets in the Annual Budget for transport/communications and agriculture are projected to grow 5% and 7% per year over the 1978-1985 period; those targets are similarly below past average growth rates of 9% and 12%, respectively, over the decade 1966-1975.

Management of the Hard Currency Balance. The final set of strategic assumptions concerns the central direction of Soviet hard currency trade. We have assumed that Soviet gold production (net of domestic use) will be sold on the world market, generating an annual inflow growing from $1.5 billion in 1977 to $2.5 billion in 1985. The Soviet balance on services and transportation is projected to grow 10% per year, rising from $300 million in 1976 to $700 million in 1985. The major source of those earnings will probably be merchant shipping with a secondary source being tourism, particularly concentrated in 1980 because of the Olympics. Grain imports from the Developed West are projected to grow 2% annually from a 1978 level of $1.2 billion (approximately 8 million metric tons) through 1985. The remainder of the Soviet deficit on current account will be covered by credit drawings in the West rising from $4.2 billion to $6.6 billion in 1985; because of the more rapid increase in repayments projected, the net capital inflow will decline from $2.2 billion in 1977 to less than $1.0 billion in 1985. Furthermore, we have assumed that Soviet leaders and Western lenders will accept a debt service ratio rising to 31% of Soviet exports to the West by 1980 and remaining at that level for the decade of the 1980s.

Modifications and Adjustments

In establishing the Baseline Solution to 1985, three different types of adjustments were introduced:

- Actual data available for 1976 and preliminary information for 1977 were imposed on the model's growth path for those years; where those adjustments were judged to have longer run significance, they were maintained for later years.

- Certain results of the model solution were modified on the basis of information provided in the 10th FYP; and

- Other adjustments were made to endogenous variables after analysis of the important balances in household accounts, foreign trade, and the State Budget.

Since all models have some weaknesses in specification, this final category of adjustments is always important. It is a major task of the analyst to recognize inconsistency in a projection and introduce appropriate adjustments. For example, the model projected a very sharp reduction in machinery imports from the West in 1976-77 because of past responses to trade deficits; because of supplemental information on Soviet orders, we augmented this category of Soviet imports to a more plausible level for the Baseline. Similarly, other trade variables were adjusted to establish greater coherence in the Soviet balances with CMEA and the Developed West. These adjustments are introduced to compensate for deficiencies in model specification or to capture more appropriately the long run movement in relative prices.

The Baseline Projection: Prospects for Soviet Growth

As we have indicated, in the preparation of this Baseline Solution analyst intervention has been confined to the imposition of actual data for 1975, adjustments for certain price changes in 1975-77, the correction of various internal and external balances, and compensation for certain deficiencies in the model itself. Consequently, this Baseline should be regarded as a potential growth path for the Soviet Union given favorable conditions in weather and the world economy. Rather than being a "forecast" of Soviet growth, it provides a standard for the construction of various scenarios; as a relatively problem-free solution,it represents the upper range of plausible outcomes.

The main indicators of the 10th FYP for 1976-1980 are compared with the Baseline Projection in Table 3.1. It is immediately apparent that the targets for industrial and agricultural output in the 10th FYP are not attained in the Baseline Solution, despite more capital investment and employment than provided in the Plan. After 1980 the Baseline indicates a smaller decline in growth rates during the 1980s than anticipated by most Western experts; the maintenance of 4% growth in GNP in the early 1980s is partially due to higher capital investment than planned during the 10th FYP and a rise in labor participation during the 11th FYP. Perhaps the Baseline's most striking feature is the stability of growth over the decade, particularly in industrial output, per capita real income, and foreign trade turnover.

The broad features of Soviet GNP growth through 1985 are presented in Table 3.2. After a rebound from the 1975 harvest failure, value-added in agriculture increases by 3% per year in the late 1970s with growth falling to 1 1/2% in the 1980s. There are modest declines in the growth rates for most other

46

TABLE 3.1
Main Indicators of Soviet Growth: Plan and Projection

INDICATORS:	Tenth Five-Year Plan	SOVMOD III Baseline	
Rates of Growth	1975-1980(1)	1975-1980(2)	1980-1985(2)
GNP	--	26.6	23.1
National Income Utilized	26.0	--	--
Industrial Output	36.0	30.9	29.2
Industrial Labor Productivity(a)	30.6	23.6	24.5
Industrial Employment(a)	4.1	5.9	3.8
Agricultural Output (5 Year Average)	16.0	12.8	15.4
Real Income per capita	21.0	15.4	15.5
New Capital Investment (5 Year Total)	25.0	30.1	23.0
Total Consumption	--	25.7	22.0
Foreign Trade Turnover (Real)	N.A.	26.9	28.1

a. For the Plan column, the employment target is derived
    implicitly from output and productivity targets. For
    projection columns, employment is determined explicitly in
    the model solution.

Sources: (1) Pravda, 30 October 1976, p. #1; (2) SOVMOD III
Projection August 1977.

TABLE 3.2
Soviet Economic Growth 1970-1985: Summary Table

| Category | Average Growth Per Annum | | |
	(1) 1970-75	(2) 1975-80	(3) 1980-85
GROSS NATIONAL PRODUCT(a)	4.1	4.8	4.2
Sectors of origin:			
Agriculture (value added)	-2.0	4.3	1.3
Industry	5.6	5.5	5.3
Construction	5.6	2.6	2.6
Transport & Communications	6.4	6.6	6.4
Domestic Trade	5.1	3.5	3.2
Services(b)	4.2	3.5	2.7
End-Use:			
Consumption: Total	3.9	4.7	4.1
: Food	2.8	3.9	3.5
: Soft Goods	4.5	5.9	5.0
: Durables	10.8	8.6	6.9
: Services	3.9	3.7	2.9
Fixed Capital Investment	4.5	4.0	4.7
Capital Repair	9.4	6.7	5.9
Other Government Expenditures	3.4	3.9	3.8

a. Value-added weights in established prices
b. Excluding military manpower

Sources: (1) See R. Greenslade, "The Real Gross National Product of the USSR, 1975", in J.E.C., op. cit., pp. 269-300 (GNP Tables in established prices provided by Greenslade); (2) and (3) Baseline Projection (August 1977), Tables 1 and 2.

sectors during the 1981-85 period. The rate of growth of construction falls sharply with the lower growth of investment and the shift toward machinery and equipment investment in the 10th FYP. The growth of transport and communications remains high and this sector grows more rapidly than industry. With the completion of the Baikal-Amur Railroad and the increased flow of Siberian resources to Pacific ports in the 1980s, freight transport should continue to grow more rapidly than industrial output. Despite above-average growth of employment in the service sector, the rate of growth of services declines because of diminished growth in non-productive capital. While the aggregate capital stock grows at an average annual rate of 6.4% over the decade, the growth rate for capital in the services sector is only 6% and the growth rate of housing capital is only 4.5%. If capital investment were reallocated to the services sector from industry and agriculture, the projected rate of growth of GNP would fall.

Foreign Trade and The Balance of Payments

The Basic Guidelines of the 10th FYP and the final document itself provide little information regarding the planned expansion of Soviet foreign trade. Given the assumptions made for world market conditions and the adjustments introduced to model equations, the Baseline supplies much more detailed information on the implied regional and commodity composition of Soviet imports and exports.

The area composition of Soviet foreign trade projected in the Baseline is presented in Table 3.3, with 1973 included as a more representative year than 1975. The share of Soviet exports going to the CMEA declines from the peak of 48.4% in 1975 but begins growing again by the late 1970s. The shares of Soviet exports to the West and to the Developing Countries grow through the late 1970s and then begin to decline. The share of Soviet imports from the CMEA rises steadily from 1975 while the share from the West peaks in 1975-76 and then declines. The share of Soviet imports from Developing Countries drops from a peak of 12% in 1975, rises again toward the end of the 10th FYP and falls during the 1980s.

In developing this Baseline, particular attention was given to regional trade balances, and particularly the hard currency balance. In Table 3.4, the major balances are indicated in millions of current dollars together with several indicators of Soviet reserves and indebtedness. The Baseline indicates a strong positive balance of the Soviet Union with

49

TABLE 3.3
Composition of Soviet Foreign Trade

A. Composition of Total Exports

Area	Actual		Baseline Projection(a)	
	1973	1975	1980	1985
CMEA	0.456	0.484	0.467	0.473
Other Socialist	0.111	0.114	0.111	0.113
Developed West	0.241	0.248	0.288	0.281
LDC's	0.091	0.096	0.103	0.102
Unspecified	0.101	0.057	0.032	0.031

B. Composition of Total Imports

Area	Actual		Baseline Projection(a)	
	1973	1975	1980	1985
CMEA	0.521	0.424	0.465	0.471
Other Socialist	0.072	0.100	0.106	0.109
Developed West	0.292	0.359	0.316	0.313
LDC's	0.115	0.117	0.113	0.107

a. Baseline Projection (August, 1977) Table 5, Appendix A.

TABLE 3.4
Soviet Trade Balances and Hard Currency Position 1975-1985
(Units=Million, Current Dollars)(a)

Year	Net Exports CMEA	Net Exports Developed West	Net Balance Hard Currency Trade	Debt Service Ratio(b)	Debt Export Ratio(c)
1975	386.	-5034.	-6281.	0.188	1.103
1976	902.	-3853.	-4315.	0.227	1.166
1977	1043.	-2216.	-2825.	0.229	1.173
1978	693.	-1656.	-2285.	0.268	1.148
1979	649.	-1251.	-1884.	0.297	1.117
1980	337.	-1326.	-2025.	0.308	1.072
1981	469.	-1608.	-2380.	0.320	1.068
1982	339.	-1404.	-2206.	0.317	1.017
1983	598.	-1558.	-2295.	0.321	0.999
1984	257.	-1861.	-2485.	0.313	0.956
1985	376.	-2636.	-3093.	0.308	0.943

a. The estimates of Soviet gold reserves, hard currency reserves and indebtedness used in the model were published in J. T. Farrell, "Soviet Payments Problems in Trade with the West", in Joint Economic Committee, Soviet Economic Prospects for the Seventies, Washington: U.S.G.P.O., 1973, pp. 690-711. An extension of this analysis appeared in J. T. Farrell and P. Ericson, "Soviet Trade and Payments with the West", in J.E.C., 1976, op. cit., pp. 727-738.
b. Debt Service Ratio = principal repayment plus interest divided by exports to the Developed West
c. Debt Export Ratio = end-year debt less hard currency reserves divided by exports to the Developed West

Source: Baseline Projection (August, 1977). Tables 5 & 6, Appendix A.

Eastern Europe primarily due to shifts in terms of trade.(11)
This surplus reaches a peak of $1.0 billion in 1977 and
remains around $0.5 billion during the rest of the decade. On
the hard currency account, the Soviet trade deficit is
projected to decline to $2.0 billion by 1980 and then rise
toward $3.0 billion by 1985. The debt service ratio rises to
30-32% by the early 1980s and then holds steady near the given
target of 31%. Even so, the ratio of external debt compared
with exports to the West declines very slowly from a peak in
1977. This suggests that Soviet credit drawings could exceed
our assumptions and that net indebtedness at the end of 1985
could be higher than the projected $22-23 billion. It should
be emphasized that this debt service measure is quite
restrictive in definition; if the net earnings on services and
gold sales are added to merchandise exports to the West, the
debt service ratio is only 27% in the 1980s.

The Baseline Solution also provides informative detail
concerning the regional and commodity composition of Soviet
foreign trade over the decade 1976-1985. In Table 3.5,
projected annual growth rates in nominal and real terms are
presented for Soviet trade with the CMEA and the West. Within
the CMEA, the shift in the terms of trade is reflected in the
4.0% annual growth in real Soviet exports compared with 6.7%
annual increase in real Soviet imports. The increases in
machinery and consumer good imports from the CMEA Six are not
surprising, but the 12% annual increase in material imports
may not be feasible. Those imports would include metallurgical
products and chemicals from Poland, East Germany, and Hungary.
In Soviet trade with the West, there is a clear suggestion of
import restraint with real imports of machinery virtually
unchanged over the decade. Among Soviet exports to the West,
the most rapid growth is projected to occur in machinery and
non-fuel materials, 10% and 6% growth in real terms. The
growth of fuel exports is quite modest at 4% per year in
volume. Soviet imports of manufactured consumer goods from
the West grow more rapidly than the comparable category of
exports.

According to this Baseline, the composition of Soviet
exports in the 1980s will not be significantly different from
that observed in the 1970s. In 1985, 74% of the value of
Soviet exports to the West will be fuel and materials compared
with 72% in 1975. Similarly, 60% of the value of Soviet
exports to the CMEA in 1985 are accounted for by raw
materials, unchanged from the level of 1975. Within the CMEA,

----

(11) Martin J. Kohn, "Development in Soviet-Eastern European
     Terms of Trade, 1971-1975, Ibid., pp. 67-80.

TABLE 3.5
The Changing Composition of Soviet Foreign Trade with the CMEA
and the West, 1976-1985

	Annual Growth Rates, 1976-85	
	Nominal	Real
Soviet Exports to the CMEA	9.7	4.0
Raw Materials	9.6	4.4
Machinery	11.4	6.4
Grain	-1.1	-3.1
Consumption Goods	1.2	-0.8
Soviet Imports from the CMEA	9.9	6.7
Raw Materials	17.6	12.0
Machinery	9.8	5.6
Food	4.1	2.1
Consumption Goods	10.4	8.2
Soviet Exports to the West	11.3	5.0
Machinery	16.9	10.1
Fuels	11.4	4.1
Other Materials	12.4	6.1
Food	6.4	2.3
Consumer Goods	9.0	4.8
Soviet Imports from the West	7.2	1.6
Machinery	5.9	-0.2
Raw Materials	9.8	3.7
Grain	-3.2	-6.1
Consumer Goods	10.1	5.8

Source: SOVMOD III Projection, August 1977; Nominal Trade:
Table 5, Appendix A; External Price Assumptions: Table 12,
Appendix A.

the USSR will benefit from the terms-of-trade shift with
rising volumes of manufactured imports from Eastern Europe.
The distinctive features in the hard currency sector are the
restraint on machinery imports that is necessary to control
the deficit on current account, given an inadequate 5% annual
growth in the volume of Soviet exports.

ALTERNATIVES TO THE BASELINE SOLUTION

The Baseline Solution described in the last section
should be regarded as an indicator of Soviet growth potential,
excluding major disturbances or crises. In particular, there
are three areas where many Western specialists would regard
the Baseline as too optimistic for Soviet growth: (1) the use
of an abnormally favorable period as the norm for future
weather conditions; (2) the projection of stable and rapid
growth for the world economy; and (3) the abstraction from any
energy crunch in the 1980's due to a stagnation in Soviet oil
production. In the first scenario presented in this section,
we will evaluate the impact of less favorable weather and a
more restrictive world economy on Soviet growth and foreign
trade. In the second scenario the impact of a Soviet oil
shortage on Soviet debt and trade will be assessed.

Scenario I: An Alternative Path with Less Favorable Weather And a More Restrictive World Economy

The issues of climatic change and food shortages became
quite prominent during the mid-1970's after harvest failures
in many regions of the world. The central argument which
emerged was that the period from 1966 to 1973 was abnormal in
two major respects: (1) weather conditions were particularly
favorable for grain production, with spring-summer
precipitation above normal and temperature below normal, and
(2) these conditions were unusually stable from year to year.
Available evidence was generally supportive of those
arguments, but the statistics were not conclusive on either
the causes of the "abnormality" or the likely consequences for
future grain production.(12)

In the wake of this discussion, a major study of the
impact of climate change on Soviet grain production was
published by the Central Intelligence Agency. It concluded
that the "severe drought of 1975 may have marked the end of
the favorable climate trend", and that the most realistic

----

(12)
    A useful review of the evidence is provided in Stephen H.
    Schneider, The Genesis Strategy (New York, 1976).

projection for average Soviet grain production over the 10th FYP would be 200 million metric tons.(13) This would represent a 10-15% shortfall from domestic grain requirements and would require substantial grain imports and a reduction of Plan goals for livestock inventories and meat output. The harvest was good in 1976 but below normal in 1977, so this bleak analysis may still be valid in the longer term. We have followed the C.I.A. suggestion for a lower estimate of "normal" weather by calculating average values for precipitation and temperature over the period 1959-1965, before the "favorable period," and using those values for 1978-1985. A comparison of Baseline and Scenario I assumptions is presented in Table 3.6.

For the world economy, we now assume slower growth in the West and lower rates of world inflation. World prices for fuel, raw materials, and gold are projected to rise less rapidly; partly as a consequence, lower growth rates are projected for the trade of developing countries. Furthermore, the rate of economic growth in Eastern Europe is assumed to be lower in this more restrictive environment. These conditions reduce Soviet hard currency earnings and Soviet exports to the CMEA; within SOVMOD III, these restrictions on exports eventually retard the growth of real Soviet machinery imports and have a small impact on Soviet industrial growth to 1985.

Given these less favorable circumstances, Soviet behavior is shifted toward increased imports of grain and toward financing of the enlarged deficit through larger gold sales and credit drawings over the period 1978-1985. The weakness of gold prices in the Alternative Projection is partly due to the lower world inflation and partly due to larger Soviet gold sales. Grain prices are projected to rise more rapidly because of less favorable weather elsewhere and Soviet grain purchases.

Scenario I is compared with the Baseline in Tables 3.7 and 3.8. The major impact on the domestic economy appears in the agricultural sector where the less favorable weather reduces the growth rate of agricultural output by approximately one percentage point per year over the decade. The impact on crop production is evident by the late 1970s with annual grain production down by 10 million tons. By the 1980s, this reduced performance in crops sharply restricts the

----

(13)
   Central Intelligence Agency, USSR: The Impact of Recent Climate Change on Grain Production, ER 76-10577 U, October 1976.

TABLE 3.6
A Comparison of Baseline and Scenario I Assumptions

===

		Assumptions, 1978-1985	
Exogenous Variables		Baseline	Scenario I
1) Weather Conditions			
Spring-Summer Precipitation	Level	0.0	-0.2743
Winter Precipitation	"	0.0	-0.1143
Winter Temperature	"	0.0	-0.0114
2) World Economy			
Industrial Production, West	Growth	5%	4%
Western Real Imports of Fuel and Materials	"	7%	5%
Real Imports of LDC's	"	7%	5%
Net Material Product, CMEA	"	6.5%	5.5%
US Price of Imported Fuel and Materials	"	7%	5%
World Grain Price	"	2%	3%
World Price of Gold	"	3%	1%
3) Soviet Decisions			
Grain Imports from the West	1978 Level	$1.2 B	$1.8 B
	Growth	2%	3%
Gold Sales	Increment	$100m per year	8%
Credit Drawings	Increment	$300m per year	8%

TABLE 3.7
A Comparison of the Baseline and Scenario I Growth Rates

	Baseline		Scenario I	
Annual Growth Rates	1976-80	1981-85	1976-80	1981-85
GNP	4.83	4.24	4.56	4.05
Industrial Output	5.54	5.26	5.48	5.17
Agricultural Output	4.68	2.50	3.50	1.54
Consumption	4.69	4.06	4.65	3.88
Fixed Capital Investment	4.01	4.69	3.59	4.18
Livestock Herd	2.08	2.86	1.39	0.59
Exports to the Developed West(a)	14.00	8.65	13.66	8.53
Imports from the Developed West(a)	5.32	9.17	6.09	8.33
Total Exports(a)	10.67	9.21	10.17	8.61
Total Imports(a)	8.08	9.33	8.06	8.57

a.   Growth in nominal trade (current dollars).

TABLE 3.8
End-Year Results: Baseline vs. Scenario I

	Baseline		Scenario I	
	1980	1985	1980	1985
Levels (Billion 1970 Rubles)				
GNP	592.4	729.1	584.9	713.3
Industrial Output	273.1	352.8	272.4	350.5
Agricultural Output	101.7	115.1	96.1	103.7
Consumption	338.1	412.6	337.6	408.3
New Capital Investment	140.1	176.2	137.3	168.5
Levels				
Grain Production (Million Metric Tons)	229.4	258.0	218.5	224.6
Gold Stock (Tons)	1974.	2034.	1897.	1690.
Trade Levels (Million Current Dollars)				
Net Exports, World	552.	411.	-647.	-805.
Net Exports, CMEA	337.	376.	369.	-158.
Net Exports, West	-1326.	-2636.	-1869.	-3074.
External Debt	16951.	22257.	17236.	22324.
Hard Currency Position	-39.	-367.	-1152.	-3002.
Debt Service Ratio	0.308	0.308	0.316	0.315
Net Debt Ratio	1.072	0.943	1.177	1.077

growth of livestock and animal production; the livestock herd grows only 0.6% per year in the 1980s compared to the nearly 3% annual growth in the Baseline. During the late 1970s the major burden of the reduction in GNP falls upon capital investment and the accumulation of livestock. During the 1980s, the impact on light industry and consumption becomes more significant but remains less than the reduction in accumulation.

In the foreign trade sector, the increase in grain imports (approximately 4 million tons and $0.6 billion in 1976 prices) and the terms-of-trade shift against the Soviet Union increase the annual deficit with the West by about $0.5 billion. The impact on the CMEA balance is smaller but grows to $0.5 billion by the mid-1980s. Total net indebtedness to the West (debt minus hard currency reserves) has increased over the Baseline by $1.4 billion at the end of 1980 and by $2.7 billion at the end of 1985. Similarly, the debt service ratio is pushed beyond the target level of 31% and the net debt ratio increases by 10%.

This less favorable external environment does not generate a major crisis for the Soviet Union. Though the reduction in consumption is modest when measured in established prices, there would be a larger reduction in consumer welfare because of the lower production of meat and processed foods. In the long run, the consequences are more serious given the lower path for sustainable growth in consumption in the 1980s due to the lower rate of capital and livestock accumulation over the decade. The adjustments in foreign trade, as projected by the model, result in only a modest 10% boost in indebtedness over the Baseline level by 1985.

Scenario II: Stagnation in Soviet Oil Production 1980s

In 1977, the Central Intelligence Agency issued a series of research reports forecasting a downturn in Soviet oil production by the 1980's and exploring its implications for the world energy balance and Soviet growth prospects.(14)

----

(14)
This analysis was published in four research papers by the Central Intelligence Agency: (1) "The International Energy Situation: Outlook to 1985," ER77-10240U, April 1977; (2) "Prospects for Soviet Oil Production,"

Their analysis was based upon detailed study of the major petroleum fields and extraction methodologies. Their major conclusions were (1) the maximum level of output of 11-12 million barrels per day (mb/d) could not be sustained during the mid-1980's; (2) the USSR's hard currency earnings from sales of crude oil would fall sharply in the 1980's; and (3) the CMEA would become a net importer of OPEC oil.

In evaluating the consequences of an oil shortage for the Soviet Union, we wish to go beyond the technological problems to a consideration of indirect effects and policy responses.(15) The first step in our analysis is a reduction of the projected growth rate for the petroleum and gas industry as indicated in Table 3.9 below. The baseline projection of 6.8% growth through 1980 and 5.8% growth in the 1980s (based on factor inputs only) has been reduced to 4.2% to 1980 and to 2.2% in the 1980s. This represents stagnation in crude oil production in the 1980s, small growth in refined petroleum products, and 7-8% annual growth in natural gas. The major indirect effects of the oil shortage on domestic production were assumed to occur in the branch of chemicals and petrochemicals (a reduction of 0.8% in the annual growth rate) and machine-building and metal-working (a reduction of 0.9% in the annual growth rate). These assumptions were based on the importance of petroleum as a raw material in the chemicals branch and the need to manufacture machinery which is more efficient in energy use. Exports of fuel to the West were reduced an average of $1.5 billion over the period 1980-85 and exports of raw materials to the CMEA were also reduced an average of $1.5 billion over the period 1980-85.

In a second stage of policy response to the impending oil shortage, capital investment in the petroleum branch is augmented by 500 million rubles each year from 1977 to 1985. Annual investment in the coal industry is also raised by 100

ER77-10270, April 1977; (3) "Prospects for Soviet Oil Production: A Supplemental Analysis," ER77-10425, July 1977; and (4) "Soviet Economic Problems and Prospects," ER 77-10436U, July 1977.

(15)
    This Scenario II is examined in greater detail in Green and Levine, The Soviet Economy in the 1980s, Chapter 3.

TABLE 3.9
The Growth of Petroleum and Gas Production, 1976-1985(a)

Period	Mean Annual Growth Rates		
	Baseline	Partial Adjustment	Final Scenario
1976-1985	6.25%	3.07%	3.91%
1976-1980	6.79%	4.16%	5.30%
1981-1985	5.81%	2.21%	2.78%

a. The final scenario result integrates both the partial
    adjustment downward on petroleum output and the expansion
    in capacity resulting from higher capital investment and
    machinery imports from 1977 onwards.

million rubles over the same period. Annual imports of Western oil equipment are raised by 500 million rubles ($670 million), one-half of which is added to total machinery imports from the West and one-half of which is substituted for other machinery. This burst of machinery imports is limited to the six years 1977-1982.

The third stage of the analysis involves the responses embedded in the model itself. The deterioration of the hard currency trade deficit (due to machinery imports and reduced fuel exports) results in a reduction of other imports from the West (raw materials particularly) and increases in exports of other raw materials. The surge of capital investment and imported machinery results in an expansion of petroleum capacity after a lag of several years. As a consequence, the annual real growth in petroleum and gas rebounds to 2.8%.

We should emphasize that the results of Scenario II will not be as abrupt as the implications of the C.I.A. study for a number of reasons:

- we have assumed stagnation in Soviet oil production during the 1980s rather than a sharp decline;

- we assume lower growth for oil consumption in the USSR and Eastern Europe;

- we have introduced an explicit policy to expand capacity in petroleum and coal to reduce the shortfall in energy; and

- we have concentrated the indirect effect on Soviet GNP on the two important branches of chemicals and machine-building.

Furthermore, by using the macroeconometric model we have included plausible responses in Soviet behavior to the deterioration in the balance of payments. While generally our projection indicates more rapid growth in the Soviet economy than does the C.I.A.'s analysis, the crucial issue is the impact of the energy crisis on the rate of economic growth.

In Table 3.10 below, we have compared the Baseline with Scenario II. While the impact of the oil shortage is not as dramatic as indicated in the CIA study, it still remains quite significant. In the 1980s, the GNP growth rate falls by nearly 0.4% to 3.8%. Given the otherwise favorable assumptions made in the scenario, this is quite close to the upper range of the CIA's "prompt action" projection (3 to 3.5%). The impact on the industrial growth rate in the 1980s

TABLE 3.10
A Comparison of the Baseline Solution and Scenario II

Category	Baseline		Scenario II	
	1976–80	1981–85	1976–80	1981–85
Annual Growth Rates:				
GNP	4.83	4.24	4.72	3.84
Industrial Output	5.54	5.26	5.30	4.46
Petroleum & Gas	6.27	5.81	5.08	2.78
Coal Production	1.96	1.59	2.09	2.25
Consumption	4.69	4.06	4.44	3.26
Exports of Fuel to DW(a)	14.70	8.15	14.50	2.19
Total Exports to DW(a)	14.00	8.65	13.94	5.66
Total Imports from DW(a)	5.32	9.17	5.93	4.88
	1980	1985	1980	1985
Levels (Billion 1970 Rubles)				
GNP	592.4	729.1	589.3	711.6
Consumption	338.1	412.6	334.1	392.3
Real Disposable Income	269.0	326.2	266.8	313.5
New Capital Investment	140.1	176.2	143.6	184.5
Levels (Million Current Dollars)				
NET Exports, CMEA	337.	376.	202.	-550.
NET Exports, DW	-1326.	-2636.	-1868.	-1609.
Exports of Fuel, DW	8579.	12696.	8504.	9475.
Imports of Machinery, DW	5743.	8970.	6352.	7892.
External Debt	16990.	22624.	18455.	24610.
Debt Service Ratio	0.308	0.308	0.309	0.396

a. In current dollars.

is even more pronounced, dropping 0.8% to 4 1/2% due to the direct and indirect impacts of the oil shortage. The impact on the growth of consumption is larger than on GNP because of the increased burden of capital investment in the fuel sectors. The growth of coal production in the 1980s has also been raised because of greater capital investment.

The most interesting features of the scenario concern the impacts on Soviet foreign trade and hard currency indebtedness. Within the CMEA the constraints on Soviet exports of fuel reduce Soviet net exports by $900 million by 1985, turning the projected surplus of $376 million to a deficit of $550 million. Instead of the Baseline annual growth in Soviet-CMEA trade turnover of 9.6% from 1980 to 1985, Scenario II indicates annual growth of 8.6%.

With the emphasis on Western petroleum equipment, Soviet imports from the West grow more rapidly to 1980 in Scenario II. Thereafter, the lower growth in export earnings due to the oil shortage eventually restrains import growth below 5% during the 1980s. Given the assumption of 7% growth in fuel prices, the projections of 2% growth in Soviet nominal exports of fuel represents a fall of 5% annually in volume. The trade deficit with the West actually declines from the Baseline level in the 1980s because of the import restrictions stimulated by a rising debt service burden. Although Soviet indebtednesss is only $2.0 billion above the Baseline by 1985, the debt service burden has been pushed to 40% of the value of exports to the West, considerably above the target of 31%.

In our judgment, the C.I.A.'s analysis of Soviet oil prospects and the consequences for Soviet GNP growth probably exaggerates the impending slowdown. Still, using our model and assumptions, we observe an impact on Soviet growth and trade which is very significant. In summary, an oil shortage of this magnitude in the 1980s would:

- reduce annual growth of Soviet GNP by 0.5% (lowering projected growth to 3.5 to 4% in the 1980s);

- reduce annual industrial growth in the USSR by 1% (to around 4.5% in the 1980s);

- eliminate the Soviet Union's projected trade surplus with the CMEA by the early 1980s;

- force a sharp reduction in the growth of Soviet imports from the West in the 1980s because of the burden of debt acquired during the 1974-76 period; and

64

- reduce the sustainable growth of consumption by 1 percentage point unless defense and investment commitments are reduced in the 1980s.

THE IMPLICATIONS FOR THE SOVIET UNION'S ROLE IN THE WORLD ECONOMY OF THE 1980S

By presenting the Baseline Solution and two major scenarios to 1985 we have attempted to identify the range of plausible outcomes for Soviet economic growth and the development of Soviet foreign trade. In our judgment, the most likely outcomes will fall in the range where Soviet GNP growth is 3.5 to 4% annually through 1985 and the annual growth rate of Soviet real foreign trade is 4.5 to 5%. This rate of economic growth should be sufficient for meeting domestic goals and foreign obligations:

- real defense expenditures rising 4%;

- per capita consumption rising 2 to 2.5%;

- capital investment rising 3.5 to 4%;

- progress in developing Siberian resources for export growth in the late 1980s; and

- establishing stability in the debt to export ratio by 1980.

This prognosis does not mean that growth will be steady and uneventful. In fact, one should expect harvest problems one year out of every three, a major harvest failure sometime during the decade, and recurrent shortages and bottlenecks along the path. However, the resource foundation of Soviet growth appears secure and the adaptability of the economic system is greater than generally acknowledged in the West.

The major vulnerabilities of the Soviet economy have been considered in our two Scenarios. Even should such adverse circumstances be combined, we would still not expect Soviet GNP growth rates to fall below 3% during the early 1980s. These adverse circumstancces would, however, cause serious problems for certain sectors of the economy. The less favorable weather conditions of Scenario I reduce agricultural growth from 2.5% to 1.5% in the 1980s; this has a significant impact on the growth of livestock and meat production. However, Soviet heavy industry could maintain a rapid growth rate and higher grain imports could be financed with a modest rise in Western credits. The energy situation in Scenario II has a larger impact on Soviet industrial growth and the hard currency situation. The restrictions imposed on hard currency trade in that Scenario result in a sharp rise in the debt service burden by the 1980s. Those prospects might well stimulate a more vigorous response in the Soviet Union than that indicated by the Scenario's modest "energy program" and the regular bureaucratic responses indicated by the econometric model.

In reviewing the foreign trade implications of these simulations, there are several dominant characteristics. First, foreign trade will become more important relative to the Soviet economy by the 1980s but there is little prospect for a significant change in the degree of trade dependence. As long as the Soviet Union retains access to the world markets for grain, machinery and credit, shifts in world economic conditions will not have a dramatic impact on Soviet economic growth. The Soviet Union remains much more independent of world economic trends than the West and East European nations, Japan and the Developing Countries. This rather unique situation will tend to promote political as well as economic stability in the Soviet Union during the 1980s.

Second, the composition of Soviet foreign trade in the 1980s will not be very different from what it was in the 1970s. Even in the circumstances of an oil shortage in Scenario II, the proportion of fuels and materials in total exports in 1985 is still 58% for CMEA trade and 70% for trade with the West (compared with 60% and 74% in the Baseline). The Soviet Union's comparative advantage in the production and export of raw materials will persist indefinitely and should help finance the selective upgrading of Soviet manufacturing technology to world standards.

Third, the Baseline Solution indicates much lower growth in Soviet imports from the West during the decade to 1985; this restraint on imports from the West, particularly machinery, is intensified in the two Scenarios. This restraint on imports derives from two sources: (1) the declining growth rate for Soviet hard currency exports (falling from 14% to 9% annually in the Baseline), and (2) the effort to establish stability in the debt service ratio at 31% in the 1980s. A relaxation of either of those constraints would expand the Soviet market for Western machinery and other manufactures.

The implications of this quantitative assessment for institutional developments within the Soviet Union, given the wider context of domestic and international politics, can only

66

be sketched briefly here.(16) The fundamental determinant of Soviet adaptation and participation in the world economy is the political commitment by the Communist Party to such an extended role. It is important to emphasize that current Soviet interest in such a role is a quite recent phenomenon of the Brezhnev period, and that the depth of Soviet involvement in world trade is qualitatively different from previous Russian forays into Western markets. It is difficult to judge the security of this commitment of the Party to deeper economic relations with the West. There have been dissents to this policy shift within the Soviet Union, not only within the Party itself but also within parts of the scientific establishment. To the extent that this commitment rests upon economic gain, we feel that it should be secure for some time. The policy appears to have made a significant contribution to Soviet industrial growth, resulting both from a selective policy of foreign imports and a modification of resource allocation within the Soviet Union. However, judgment based upon economic interest may be ultimately reversed on political or ideological grounds. We would stress that a Soviet withdrawal, if it should occur, would probably mean a return to a passive short run exchange of commodities on the world market rather than a retreat to isolation.

Since we anticipate a slowdown in the growth of Soviet trade with the West there exists no "imperative" for Soviet economic institutions to change in a dramatic fashion. For example, the Soviet emphasis upon longterm compensation agreements actually tends to shift the responsibility for marketing of Soviet exports to Western firms. Given their longterm and bilateral character, such forms of foreign trade are much less disruptive to the established Foreign Trade Organizations. Compensation agreements involving manufactured goods do impose new obligations on Soviet producers to meet world market standards, but the Western partner becomes the source of technological upgrading and new product development. The establishment of an export sector of specialized firms, which has been suggested by Premier Kosygin, would also minimize the disruption of traditional organizations within the economy.

We further expect that Soviet economic relations with the West will continue to have a strong bilateral flavor during the 1980s. There are certain economic advantages to the USSR of dealing bilaterally with Western economies, although these

----

(16)
    A more ambitious treatment of these issues appears in Ibid., Chapter 4.

advantages have often been exaggerated in Western political circles and the Western press. The major force for bilateralism within the Soviet Union, however, arises from Soviet political structure and attitudes. The emphasis upon the economic role of the Party establishes a strong bias for a political intergovernmental framework of negotiations. Such large economic transactions are viewed as an integral part of Soviet foreign policy, and thus are scheduled to coincide with meetings of top leaders. This political visibility of Party and government officials also helps to legitimate such transactions with Western capitalism for the Party and military apparatus, generally suspicious of all commercial activity. A final political rationale for bilateralism derives from traditional Russian feelings of inferiority with respect to the West. If economic relations are going to have a political dimension, the Soviet Union is much more comfortable negotiating with France or Germany than with the European Economic Community. This consciousness of relative scale in the world economy is a serious barrier to Soviet participation in multilateral institutions dominated by the Developed West.

Although we expect Soviet economic relations with the West to continue through bilateral institutions, there is the likelihood that the USSR will consider enlarged participation in multilateral institutions. During the euphoric days of detente and East-West trade expansion there was serious consideration, at least in the West, of eventual Soviet membership in the leading multilateral institutions developed for cooperation of Western market economies -- the General Agreement on Tariffs and Treaties (GATT), the International Monetary Fund (IMF), and the World Bank. With the anticipated slowdown in East-West trade in the late 1970s and a renewed Soviet interest in the potentials of CMEA institutions, those issues are no longer as urgent as they once appeared.

The major impediments to the participation of planned socialist economies in multilateral institutions, developed for cooperation among market capitalist economies, remain reciprocal accessibility and currency convertibility.(17) The

----

(17)
   These issues have been addressed in a useful paper by William Diebold, Jr., "The Communist Countries in the World Economy of the 1980s," Draft Paper, Council on Foreign Relations, June 1976. The issue of ruble convertibility is discussed in Adam Zwass, Monetary Cooperation Between East and West (White Plains, New York: International Arts and Sciences Press, 1975), and Lawrence

inclusion of the Soviet Union within the framework of GATT cannot be ruled out, given the ambiguity of the rules for State trading agencies, and might serve as a quid pro quo for the granting of MFN status by the United States. Some formalization of East-West trading procedures through the auspices of GATT would be acceptable to the Soviet Union as long as it did not interfere with the existing pattern of long term bilateral trade agreements. The participation of the Soviet Union in the IMF and World Bank would, however, be unlikely without a substantial revision of the rules of those organizations to accomodate the centrally-planned systems. Certainly, the current voting arrangements of the Fund which provide control by a minority of large Western economies would pose a serious block to Soviet participation. Should the IMF or other Western monetary institutions become active in the regulation of international banking, and the Eurocurrency market in particular, Soviet interest in participating in those organizations might develop very rapidly.

During the past decade, the importance of the CMEA market to the USSR was partially eclipsed by the political priority given to promoting East-West trade and technology transfer. For a number of important reasons, the pendulum appears to have swung back toward renewed interest in the potential development of the CMEA itself. First, the shift in relative prices during the 1970s and the strains on Soviet capacity in many extractive industries have become a major force for CMEA economic integration through rising real CMEA exports to the Soviet Union and the introduction of CMEA joint investment projects. Second, the difficulties faced by East European and Soviet exporters to the West increase the importance of CMEA markets and intra-CMEA cooperation. A third source of pressure arises in the political sphere, with Communist Parties in Eastern Europe concerned about political unity given the post-Helsinki environment, ideological problems of Eurocommunism in the West, and declining growth prospects in central Europe, particularly in the German Democratic Republic, Czechoslovakia and Hungary.

The increased volume of intra-CMEA trade and the problems of domestic growth in Eastern Europe will intensify the pressure for organizational change within CMEA. Without attempting an extensive review of CMEA institutional development and problems, we can anticipate growing debate

----

J. Brainard, "The CMEA Financial System and Integration," in Paul Marer and J. M. Montias (eds.), Eastern European Integration and East-West Trade (Bloomington, Ind.: 1977).

during the late 1970s on the following issues: long run joint planning and development projects, industrial cooperation in manufacturing, price determination and flexibility, and monetary integration.(18)

During the 31st CMEA Council session in 1977, the major topic was long run economic cooperation in the fields of fuel, energy, and raw materials. The second level of CMEA integration, cooperation agreements and joint production by CMEA enterprises, may be as significant as the large energy projects over the next decade. Given a relaxation in bilateralism, these arrangements would be sought actively by enterprises and associations to promote the exchange of technology and extend market size. Organizational development in this area could also promote the diffusion of Western technology already absorbed by enterprises in the USSR, Hungary, Poland, etc.

The CMEA price system will be another institutional area which will be subject to pressure for reform. In 1975, the CMEA accepted a five-year moving average of world market prices as a basis for intra-CMEA prices; this agreement was an ad hoc adjustment to the dramatic shift in world prices which took place in 1973-1974. The most promising directions for reform in CMEA pricing would appear to be (1) a departure from equal weights in determining the moving average for "official" prices, and (2) the provision of greater price flexibility in contracts between associations. A further area of CMEA organizational change may involve convertibility of the transferable ruble (TR) and monetary integration within the group. In a period when the USSR expects to generate substantial surpluses on its clearing accounts with the CMEA Six, there may be better prospects of monetary reform than in the past.

There are many potential directions of monetary reform in CMEA, but two developments would appear most promising. First, economic associations active in intra-CMEA trade could be allowed to hold multilateral accounts with the International Bank for Economic Cooperation (IBEC), the Moscow-based clearing bank; this would promote the long run development of cooperation between associations, reduce many bureaucratic barriers to mutually-advantageous trade, and

----

(18)

    On the organization and prospects of CMEA integration, a recent study is Jozef M. P. Van Brabant, _Eastern European Cooperation: The Role of Money and Finance_ (New York: Praeger, 1977).

support the liberalization of intra-CMEA pricing. Second, IBEC could establish convertibility for some proportion of official deposits by member countries. Superficially, intra-CMEA trade in convertible currencies could then be recorded in multilateral TRs. With the adoption of more active borrowing in the West, the IBEC could improve hard currency liquidity within the CMEA and provide multilateral support to countries experiencing balance-of-payments problems. In certain areas such as foreign borrowing, there are political advantages for the USSR in using CMEA banks to provide distance from the issues of indebtedness to the West. The CMEA International Investment Bank (IIB) has already taken a more prominent role in the financing of the Orenburg pipeline. This project may serve as the prototype for future development of Soviet petroleum resources and other materials in the 1980s. Western technology, machinery and required materials (e.g., large diameter pipe) would be financed by Western credits to the IIB and repaid through future export earnings by the USSR.

SRI-WEFA ECONOMETRIC MODEL OF THE SOVIET UNION
BASELINE FOR CFR STUDY (11/9/77)

TABLE 1.00 GNP BY SECTOR-OF-ORIGIN

ITEM	1975	1976	1977	1978	1979	1980
GNP, SECTOR-OF-ORIGIN, B.1970R----	468,018	488,027	515,822	543,046	565,291	592,396
PERCENTAGE GROWTH IN GNP----	2.74	4.28	5.70	5.28	4.10	4.79
GNP PER CAPITA, 1970 RB/PERSON----	1831,771	1892,310	1980,884	2065,638	2127,151	2207,223
GROWTH IN GNP PER CAPITA----	1.86	3.30	4.68	4.18	3.08	3.76
GNP, SECTOR-OF-ORIGIN, B.1970R						
AGRICULTURE----	64,683	68,030	73,016	76,868	76,584	79,678
-GROWTH----	-11.01	5.18	7.33	5.28	-0.37	4.04
INDUSTRY----	208,585	218,418	231,726	245,413	258,735	273,073
-GROWTH----	5.81	4.71	6.09	5.91	5.43	5.54
CONSTRUCTION----	33,512	33,301	34,529	35,734	36,693	37,801
-GROWTH----	7.60	-0.03	3.69	3.49	2.68	3.02
TRANSPORT/COMMUNICATION----	43,016	46,227	49,302	52,491	55,835	59,277
-GROWTH----	6.24	7.46	6.65	6.47	6.37	6.16
DOMESTIC TRADE----	21,322	21,666	22,488	23,443	24,395	25,275
-GROWTH----	4.19	1.61	3.79	4.25	4.06	3.61
SERVICES/GOVERNMENT----	49,816	51,330	53,258	55,193	57,183	59,039
-GROWTH----	4.10	3.04	3.76	3.63	3.61	3.25
MILITARY PERSONNEL EXPENDITURES----	6,027	6,035	6,035	6,035	6,035	6,035
-GROWTH----	4.43	0.12	0.0	0.0	0.0	0.0
NET MATERIAL PRODUCT, B.1970R----	340,846	356,419	378,300	399,506	416,078	437,255
PERCENTAGE GROWTH IN NMP----	2.33	4.57	6.14	5.61	4.15	5.09

SRI-WEFA ECONOMETRIC MODEL OF THE SOVIET UNION
BASELINE FOR CFR STUDY (11/9/77)

TABLE 1,00 GNP BY SECTOR-OF-ORIGIN

ITEM	1975	1976	1977	1978	1979	1980
GNP, INDUSTRY, 1970=100:						
TOTAL	132,76	139,01	147,48	156,20	164,67	175,80
BY BRANCH:						
ELECTROENERGY	140,25	149,45	158,65	167,67	176,60	186,47
COAL PRODUCTS	110,82	115,89	116,26	118,13	119,81	122,10
PETROLEUM PRODUCTS	141,20	147,15	158,23	169,63	179,94	191,40
FERROUS METALLURGY	120,85	126,86	131,51	136,11	140,68	145,45
NON-FERROUS METALLURGY	127,73	130,75	136,04	141,59	147,67	153,61
CONSTRUCTION MATERIALS	128,87	133,44	139,63	146,04	152,30	158,94
CHEMICALS & PETROCHEMICALS	152,69	162,84	176,74	191,83	208,59	226,56
MACHINE BLDG.&METAL WRKG,	154,29	168,14	182,74	198,11	214,16	230,71
FOREST PRODUCTS	111,33	113,11	115,50	118,01	119,97	122,30
PAPER & PULP	125,90	130,85	136,34	142,45	148,07	154,53
SOFT GOODS	114,28	117,20	121,99	126,22	128,43	131,70
PROCESSED FOODS	120,76	121,12	126,27	131,57	136,61	142,08
GNP, INDUSTRIAL BRANCH GROWTH RATES						
ELECTROENERGY	6,35	6,56	6,16	5,68	5,33	5,59
COAL PRODUCTS	2,34	2,77	2,07	1,61	1,43	1,91
PETROLEUM PRODUCTS	7,15	4,21	7,53	7,21	6,08	6,37
FERROUS METALLURGY	4,91	4,97	3,67	3,49	3,36	3,39
NON-FERROUS METALLURGY	5,00	2,37	4,04	4,08	4,30	4,02
CONSTRUCTION MATERIALS	4,65	3,54	4,64	4,59	4,28	4,36
CHEMICALS & PETROCHEMICALS	11,29	6,65	8,54	8,54	8,74	8,62
MACHINE BLDG.&METAL WRKG,	8,04	8,98	8,68	8,41	8,10	7,75
FOREST PRODUCTS	4,21	1,60	2,12	2,17	1,66	1,95
PAPER & PULP	4,78	3,93	4,19	4,48	3,95	4,57
SOFT GOODS	2,41	2,56	4,04	3,51	1,75	2,55
PROCESSED FOODS	3,83	0,30	4,25	4,20	3,83	4,00

SRI-WEFA ECONOMETRIC MODEL OF THE SOVIET UNION
BASELINE FOR CFR STUDY (11/9/77)

TABLE   1.00 GNP BY SECTOR-OF-ORIGIN

ITEM	1975	1976	1977	1978	1979	1980
SHARES OF SECTORS IN GNP						
AGRICULTURE	0.138	0.139	0.142	0.142	0.135	0.135
INDUSTRY	0.461	0.448	0.449	0.452	0.458	0.461
CONSTRUCTION	0.071	0.068	0.067	0.066	0.065	0.064
TRANSPORT/COMMUNICATION	0.092	0.095	0.096	0.097	0.099	0.100
DOMESTIC TRADE	0.046	0.044	0.044	0.043	0.043	0.043
SERVICES/GOVERNMENT	0.106	0.105	0.103	0.102	0.101	0.100
MIL. PERSONNEL EXP.	0.013	0.012	0.012	0.011	0.011	0.010
UNALLOCATED	0.088	0.088	0.088	0.088	0.088	0.088
SHARES OF END-USE CATEGORIES IN GNP						
CONSUMPTION	0.575	0.568	0.568	0.568	0.571	0.571
INVESTMENT	0.357	0.355	0.355	0.355	0.354	0.356
GOVERNMENT	0.120	0.119	0.117	0.116	0.116	0.115
NET EXPORTS	-0.027	-0.023	-0.020	-0.020	-0.021	-0.021
END-USE RESIDUAL	-0.025	-0.019	-0.020	-0.020	-0.020	-0.021
SHARES OF BRANCHES IN INDUSTRY GNP:						
ELECTROENERGY	0.049	0.050	0.050	0.050	0.050	0.050
COAL PRODUCTS	0.026	0.026	0.025	0.024	0.023	0.022
PETROLEUM PRODUCTS	0.063	0.063	0.064	0.065	0.065	0.066
FERROUS METALLURGY	0.048	0.048	0.047	0.046	0.045	0.044
NON-FERROUS METALLURGY	0.030	0.029	0.028	0.028	0.028	0.027
CONSTRUCTION MATERIALS	0.042	0.042	0.041	0.041	0.040	0.040
CHEMICALS & PETROCHEMICALS	0.059	0.061	0.062	0.064	0.065	0.067
MACHINE BLDG.,&METAL WRKG.	0.301	0.313	0.320	0.328	0.336	0.343
FOREST PRODUCTS	0.038	0.037	0.035	0.034	0.033	0.032
PAPER & PULP	0.007	0.007	0.007	0.007	0.007	0.007
SOFT GOODS	0.142	0.139	0.137	0.133	0.129	0.125
PROCESSED FOODS	0.151	0.144	0.142	0.140	0.138	0.136

SRI-WEFA ECONOMETRIC MODEL OF THE SOVIET UNION
BASELINE FOR CFR STUDY (11/9/77)

TABLE 1.00 GNP BY SECTOR-OF-ORIGIN

ITEM	1980	1981	1982	1983	1984	1985
GNP,SECTOR-OF-ORIGIN,B,1970R	592,396	616,291	645,122	669,163	698,749	729,143
PERCENTAGE GROWTH IN GNP	4.79	4.03	4.68	3.73	4.42	4.35
GNP PER CAPITA, 1970 RB/PERSON	2207,223	2273,631	2356,694	2420,820	2503,848	2588,756
GROWTH IN GNP PER CAPITA	3.76	3.01	3.65	2.72	3.43	3.39
GNP,SECTOR-OF-ORIGIN,B,1970R						
AGRICULTURE	79,678	79,089	82,192	81,610	84,100	85,155
-GROWTH	4.04	-0.74	3.92	-0.71	3.05	1.25
INDUSTRY	273,073	287,687	303,290	318,412	334,814	352,785
-GROWTH	5.54	5.35	5.42	4.99	5.15	5.37
CONSTRUCTION	37,801	38,751	39,891	40,745	41,804	43,050
-GROWTH	3.02	2.51	2.94	2.14	2.60	2.98
TRANSPORT/COMMUNICATION	59,277	63,153	67,064	71,098	75,864	80,773
-GROWTH	6.16	6.54	6.19	6.01	6.70	6.47
DOMESTIC TRADE	25,275	26,236	27,086	27,933	28,706	29,609
-GROWTH	3.61	3.80	3.24	3.13	2.77	3.14
SERVICES/GOVERNMENT	59,039	61,014	62,697	64,344	65,832	67,463
-GROWTH	3.25	3.34	2.76	2.63	2.31	2.48
MILITARY PERSONNEL EXPENDITURES	6,035	6,035	6,035	6,035	6,035	6,035
-GROWTH	0.0	0.0	0.0	0.0	0.0	0.0
NET MATERIAL PRODUCT, R,1970R	437,255	455,197	478,021	496,483	520,030	544,019
PERCENTAGE GROWTH IN NMP	5.09	4.10	5.01	3.86	4.74	4.61

SRI-WEFA ECONOMETRIC MODEL OF THE SOVIET UNION
BASELINE FOR CFR STUDY (11/9/77)

TABLE   1.00 GNP BY SECTOR-OF-ORIGIN

I T E M	1980	1981	1982	1983	1984	1985
GNP, INDUSTRY, 1970=100:						
TOTAL	173.80	183.10	193.03	202.66	213.10	224.53
BY BRANCH:						
ELECTROENERGY	186.47	197.01	207.88	218.44	229.40	241.71
COAL PRODUCTS	122.10	124.21	126.57	128.17	129.94	132.14
PETROLEUM PRODUCTS	191.40	202.67	215.58	227.18	240.01	253.89
FERROUS METALLURGY	145.45	150.34	155.06	159.58	164.41	169.84
NON-FERROUS METALLURGY	153.61	160.17	165.86	171.96	177.92	184.64
CONSTRUCTION MATERIALS	158.94	165.74	172.89	179.79	187.19	195.25
CHEMICALS & PETROCHEMICALS	226.56	245.28	265.57	287.37	311.41	337.24
MACHINE BLDG,&METAL WRKG,	230.71	248.15	266.00	284.39	303.51	324.26
FOREST PRODUCTS	122.30	124.42	126.80	128.40	130.39	132.83
PAPER & PULP	154.53	160.80	168.01	174.46	181.87	190.01
SOFT GOODS	131.70	134.19	138.02	140.15	143.64	147.82
PROCESSED FOODS	142.08	147.52	153.41	158.92	165.00	171.56
GNP, INDUSTRIAL BRANCH GROWTH RATES:						
ELECTROENERGY	5.59	5.65	5.52	5.08	5.02	5.37
COAL PRODUCTS	1.91	1.73	1.90	1.27	1.38	1.69
PETROLEUM PRODUCTS	6.37	5.89	6.37	5.38	5.65	5.78
FERROUS METALLURGY	3.39	3.36	3.14	2.91	3.03	3.30
NON-FERROUS METALLURGY	4.02	4.27	3.56	3.67	3.47	3.78
CONSTRUCTION MATERIALS	4.36	4.28	4.31	3.99	4.12	4.31
CHEMICALS & PETROCHEMICALS	8.62	8.26	8.27	8.21	8.37	8.30
MACHINE BLDG,&METAL WRKG,	7.73	7.56	7.19	6.91	6.72	6.84
FOREST PRODUCTS	1.95	1.73	1.91	1.26	1.55	1.87
PAPER & PULP	4.37	4.06	4.48	3.84	4.25	4.47
SOFT GOODS	2.55	1.89	2.85	1.54	2.49	2.91
PROCESSED FOODS	4.00	3.83	4.00	3.59	3.82	3.98

SRI-WEFA ECONOMETRIC MODEL OF THE SOVIET UNION
BASELINE FOR CFR STUDY (11/9/77)

TABLE   1.00 GNP BY SECTOR-OF-ORIGIN

I T E M	1980	1981	1982	1983	1984	1985
SHARES OF SECTORS IN GNP						
AGRICULTURE	0.135	0.128	0.127	0.122	0.120	0.117
INDUSTRY	0.461	0.467	0.470	0.476	0.479	0.484
CONSTRUCTION	0.064	0.063	0.062	0.061	0.060	0.059
TRANSPORT/COMMUNICATION	0.100	0.102	0.104	0.106	0.109	0.111
DOMESTIC TRADE	0.043	0.043	0.042	0.042	0.041	0.041
SERVICES/GOVERNMENT	0.100	0.099	0.097	0.096	0.094	0.093
MIL, PERSONNEL EXP,	0.010	0.010	0.009	0.009	0.009	0.008
UNALLOCATED	0.088	0.088	0.088	0.088	0.088	0.088
SHARES OF END-USE CATEGORIES IN GNP						
CONSUMPTION	0.571	0.574	0.570	0.571	0.568	0.566
INVESTMENT	0.356	0.354	0.358	0.359	0.363	0.366
GOVERNMENT	0.115	0.114	0.114	0.114	0.113	0.113
NET EXPORTS	-0.021	-0.022	-0.021	-0.022	-0.022	-0.022
END-USE RESIDUAL	-0.021	-0.021	-0.021	-0.022	-0.022	-0.022
SHARES OF BRANCHES IN INDUSTRY GNP						
ELECTROENERGY	0.050	0.050	0.050	0.050	0.050	0.050
COAL PRODUCTS	0.022	0.021	0.021	0.020	0.019	0.019
PETROLEUM PRODUCTS	0.066	0.066	0.066	0.067	0.067	0.067
FERROUS METALLURGY	0.044	0.043	0.042	0.042	0.041	0.040
NON-FERROUS METALLURGY	0.027	0.027	0.026	0.026	0.026	0.025
CONSTRUCTION MATERIALS	0.040	0.039	0.039	0.039	0.038	0.038
CHEMICALS & PETROCHEMICALS	0.067	0.069	0.071	0.073	0.076	0.078
MACHINE BLDG,&METAL WRKG,	0.343	0.350	0.356	0.364	0.368	0.373
FOREST PRODUCTS	0.032	0.031	0.030	0.029	0.028	0.027
PAPER & PULP	0.007	0.007	0.007	0.006	0.006	0.006
SOFT GOODS	0.125	0.121	0.118	0.114	0.111	0.109
PROCESSED FOODS	0.161	0.154	0.152	0.130	0.128	0.127

SRI-WEFA ECONOMETRIC MODEL OF THE SOVIET UNION
BASELINE FOR CFR STUDY (11/9/77)

TABLE 2.00 GNP BY END-USE

I T E M	1975	1976	1977	1978	1979	1980
GNP,END-USE,B,1970R	468,017	488,006	515,636	542,846	566,383	592,179
CONSUMPTION, TOTAL	268,928	277,249	292,661	308,517	323,584	338,113
FOOD	125,217	126,274	132,904	139,602	145,643	151,371
SOFT GOODS	54,910	57,831	61,631	65,623	69,403	73,126
DURABLE GOODS	23,324	25,659	27,927	30,388	32,811	35,279
ALL SERVICES	65,478	67,485	70,199	72,922	75,723	78,335
INVESTMENT, TOTAL	166,910	173,194	182,816	192,887	200,509	210,692
TOTAL NEW FIXED	115,095	120,192	125,522	130,909	134,851	140,125
AGRICULTURE	23,659	25,306	27,282	29,064	30,963	32,986
MACHINERY	7,100	7,100	7,100	7,100	7,100	7,100
CONSTRUCTION	16,559	16,559	16,559	16,559	16,559	16,559
INDUSTRY	40,771	43,824	45,746	47,719	49,677	51,866
ELECTROENERGY	3,747	4,052	4,130	4,202	4,474	4,760
COAL PRODUCTS	1,759	1,852	1,865	1,874	1,944	2,014
PETROLEUM PRODUCTS	5,651	6,125	6,412	6,722	7,056	7,417
FERROUS METALLURGY	2,893	2,967	3,281	3,648	3,671	3,702
NON-FERROUS METALLURGY	3,943	4,146	4,139	4,157	4,188	4,232
CHEMICALS & PETROCHEM	3,815	4,035	4,275	4,534	4,814	5,119
MACHINE BLDG & METAL WRKG	9,685	10,817	11,491	12,068	12,658	13,304
FOREST PRODUCTS	1,788	1,847	1,926	2,009	2,099	2,197
CONSTRUCTION MATERIALS	1,908	1,933	1,956	1,981	1,989	2,009
SOFT GOODS	1,628	1,835	1,944	2,075	2,225	2,397
PROCESSED FOODS	3,035	3,248	3,309	3,381	3,456	3,535
KOLKHOZ INDUSTRY	0,919	0,970	1,020	1,070	1,120	1,180

SRI-WEFA ECONOMETRIC MODEL OF THE SOVIET UNION
BASELINE FOR CFR STUDY (11/9/77)

TABLE 2.00 GNP BY END-USE

I T E M	1975	1976	1977	1978	1979	1980
INVESTMENT, continued						
CONSTRUCTION-----------	4,411	4,151	4,246	4,356	4,036	3,979
TRANSPORT/COMMUNICATIONS---	12,469	13,285	14,015	14,800	15,235	15,698
HOUSING----------------	16,349	16,868	17,346	17,838	18,343	18,863
SERVICES & TRADE-------	17,436	16,758	16,886	17,133	16,596	16,732
CAPITAL REPAIRS--------	28,648	30,384	32,533	34,770	37,108	39,537
NON-AGR, INVENTORY CHANGE:						
WHOLESALE & RETAIL TRADE---	1,809	2,196	1,749	1,726	1,883	2,040
OTHER-----------------	12,668	9,623	11,293	12,664	13,679	14,600
NET CHANGE IN LIVESTOCK-----	1,750	-1,834	2,209	2,240	2,358	2,227
GOVERNMENT, TOTAL-------	56,310	58,195	60,542	62,975	65,482	68,074
ADMINISTRATION---------	12,073	12,499	12,970	13,471	13,990	14,539
SCIENCE---------------	13,569	14,207	15,064	15,937	16,824	17,721
DEFENSE & STATE RESERVES-----	30,468	31,069	32,088	33,146	34,248	35,393
NET EXPORTS------------	-12,616	-11,203	-10,238	-10,737	-11,676	-12,456
TOTAL EXPORTS---------	25,025	27,975	29,632	30,732	32,106	33,531
TOTAL IMPORTS---------	37,642	39,178	39,870	41,469	43,782	45,987
END-USE RESIDUAL-------	-11,534	-9,429	-10,144	-10,816	-11,516	-12,242

SRI-WEFA ECONOMETRIC MODEL OF THE SOVIET UNION
BASELINE FOR CFR STUDY (11/9/77)

TABLE 2.00 GNP BY END-USE

ITEM	1980	1981	1982	1983	1984	1985
GNP,END-USE,B,1970R	592,179	618,074	644,889	671,435	698,525	728,894
CONSUMPTION, TOTAL	338,113	355,076	367,822	383,51?	376,59?	412,605
FOOD	151,371	158,294	162,897	169,102	173,835	179,978
SOFT GOODS	73,126	77,527	80,888	85,138	88,742	93,166
DURABLE GOODS	35,279	38,138	40,553	43,468	46,120	49,267
ALL SERVICES	78,335	81,114	83,483	85,801	87,895	90,190
INVESTMENT, TOTAL	210,692	218,985	231,069	240,863	253,405	266,682
TOTAL NEW FIXED	140,125	145,144	152,726	159,740	167,679	176,178
AGRICULTURE	32,986	35,140	37,436	39,881	42,487	45,263
MACHINERY	7,100	7,100	7,100	7,100	7,100	7,100
CONSTRUCTION	16,559	16,559	16,559	16,559	16,559	16,559
INDUSTRY	51,866	54,214	56,950	59,922	63,087	66,524
ELECTROENERGY	4,760	5,063	5,138	5,211	5,532	5,871
COAL PRODUCTS	2,014	2,082	2,077	2,070	2,132	2,193
PETROLEUM PRODUCTS	7,417	7,806	8,227	8,680	9,170	9,699
FERROUS METALLURGY	3,702	3,742	4,205	4,745	4,846	4,958
NON-FERROUS METALLURGY	4,232	4,289	4,359	4,445	4,547	4,666
CHEMICALS & PETROCHEM,	5,119	5,449	5,807	6,195	6,615	7,071
MACHINE BLDG & METAL WRKG	13,304	14,025	14,832	15,737	16,750	17,883
FOREST PRODUCTS	2,197	2,304	2,420	2,546	2,683	2,831
CONSTRUCTION MATERIALS	2,009	2,025	2,061	2,090	2,124	2,160
SOFT GOODS	2,397	2,594	2,818	3,074	3,365	3,696
PROCESSED FOODS	3,535	3,618	3,706	3,798	3,894	3,996
KOLKHOZ INDUSTRY	1,180	1,240	1,300	1,360	1,430	1,500

SRI-WEFA ECONOMETRIC MODEL OF THE SOVIET UNION
BASELINE FOR CFR STUDY (11/9/77)

TABLE 2.00 GNP BY END-USE

I T E M	1980	1981	1982	1983	1984	1985
INVESTMENT, continued						
CONSTRUCTION------------	3,979	3,913	4,303	4,403	4,657	4,925
TRANSPORT/COMMUNICATIONS----	15,698	16,192	17,206	18,333	19,043	19,815
HOUSING-----------	18,863	19,398	19,947	20,513	21,094	21,692
SERVICES & TRADE----	16,732	16,288	16,884	16,689	17,311	17,961
CAPITAL REPAIRS------	39,537	42,027	44,551	47,150	49,893	52,771
NON-AGR. INVENTORY CHANGE:						
WHOLESALE & RETAIL TRADE----	2,040	2,120	2,178	2,258	2,317	2,398
OTHER------------	14,600	15,347	16,035	16,551	17,146	18,098
NET CHANGE IN LIVESTOCK----	2,227	2,293	2,212	2,341	2,054	2,223
GOVERNMENT, TOTAL------------	68,074	70,735	73,483	76,301	79,199	82,165
ADMINISTRATION-----------	14,539	15,106	15,710	16,335	16,995	17,681
SCIENCE------------	17,721	18,624	19,530	20,433	21,331	22,219
DEFENSE & STATE RESERVES-----	35,393	36,584	37,823	39,111	40,451	41,845
NET EXPORTS-------	-12,456	-13,721	-13,699	-14,635	-15,217	-16,217
TOTAL EXPORTS-----------	33,531	35,113	36,859	38,540	40,788	42,823
TOTAL IMPORTS-----------	45,987	48,834	50,557	53,175	56,005	59,040
END-USE RESIDUAL*------	-12,242	-13,000	-13,786	-14,605	-15,455	-16,340

SRI-WEFA ECONOMETRIC MODEL OF THE SOVIET UNION
BASELINE FOR CFR STUDY (11/9/77)

TABLE 5.00 FOREIGN TRADE

I T E M	1975	1976	1977	1978	1979	1980
TOTAL EXPORTS,M,$US---	33140.	37766.	42003.	45739.	50174.	55024.
-GROWTH---	21.11	13.96	11.22	8.89	9.70	9.67
TOTAL IMPORTS,M,$US---	36942.	39668.	41983.	45413.	49864.	54471.
-GROWTH---	48.59	7.38	5.84	8.17	9.80	9.24
TOTAL NET EXPORTS,M$US	-3802.	-1902.	20.	326.	309.	552.
CMEA, M.US$						
EXPORTS,TOTAL---	16055.	17934.	19810.	21213.	23463.	25671.
RAW MATERIALS---	9645.	10473.	12019.	12776.	13947.	15284.
MACHINERY---	3566.	4563.	4740.	5161.	5941.	6564.
GRAIN---	307.	252.	226.	224.	287.	277.
CONSUMPTION GOODS---	573.	571.	542.	541.	526.	507.
UNSPECIFIED---	1964.	2075.	2283.	2511.	2762.	3038.
IMPORTS,TOTAL---	15669.	17094.	18784.	20541.	23049.	25556.
RAW MATERIALS---	1352.	1701.	2218.	2580.	3056.	3556.
MACHINERY---	7177.	8019.	8539.	9264.	10586.	11648.
FOOD---	1155.	884.	1015.	1095.	1175.	1258.
CONSUMPTION GOODS---	3057.	3339.	3704.	4129.	4585.	5065.
UNSPECIFIED---	2948.	3150.	3308.	3473.	3647.	3829.
NET EXPORTS---	386.	902.	1043.	693.	649.	557.
OTHER SOCIALIST COUNTRIES,M,$US						
EXPORTS,TOTAL---	3776.	4178.	4629.	5096.	5585.	6100.
IMPORTS,TOTAL---	3692.	3969.	4409.	4857.	5316.	5787.
NET EXPORTS---	84.	209.	220.	239.	269.	512.

SRI-WEFA ECONOMETRIC MODEL OF THE SOVIET UNION
BASELINE FOR CFH STUDY (11/9/77)

TABLE 5.00 FOREIGN TRADE

foreign trade continued

ITEM	1975	1976	1977	1978	1979	1980
DEVELOPED WEST, M.$US						
EXPORTS,TOTAL	8233.	10588.	11973.	13273.	14362.	15852.
MACHINERY	340.	459.	600.	730.	839.	977.
FUELS	4322.	5666.	6467.	7196.	7732.	8579.
OTHER MATERIALS	1576.	2257.	2449.	2637.	2831.	3079.
GRAIN	0.	0.	0.	0.	0.	0.
OTHER FOOD	227.	222.	254.	280.	299.	318.
MFG. CONSUMER GOODS	1768.	1985.	2202.	2429.	2662.	2899.
IMPORTS,TOTAL	13267.	14483.	14200.	14942.	15916.	17192.
MACHINERY	5080.	5005.	5019.	5351.	5518.	5743.
RAW MATERIALS	4666.	4552.	5226.	5990.	6556.	7336.
GRAIN	1880.	3000.	1800.	1200.	1224.	1248.
CONSUMER GOODS	1221.	1026.	1228.	1407.	1634.	1852.
UNSPECIFIED	750.	900.	927.	955.	985.	1013.
NET EXPORTS	-5034.	-3853.	-2216.	-1656.	-1251.	-1326.

SRI-WEFA ECONOMETRIC MODEL OF THE SOVIET UNION
BASELINE FOR CFR STUDY (11/9/77)

TABLE 5.00 FOREIGN TRADE

I T E M	1975	1976	1977	1978	1979	1980
(DEVELOPING COUNTRIES,M,$US						
EXPORTS,TOTAL	3172.	3866.	4272.	4705.	5167.	5661.
IMPORTS,TOTAL	4314.	4122.	4591.	5073.	5584.	6136.
NET EXPORTS	-1142.	-256.	-319.	-369.	-417.	-474.
UNSPECIFIED EXPORTS,WORLD,M,$US	1904.	1200.	1320.	1452.	1597.	1741.
MACHINERY IMPORTS						
MACH. & EQUIP.,CHEMICAL, WEST,M,$US	513.	431.	798.	957.	665.	747.
MACHINERY, METAL WORKING, TOTAL,M,C,RB	941.	959.	1119.	1281.	1409.	1581.
MACHINERY, MINING, MET,&PETROL,, TOTAL,M,C,RB	702.	829.	826.	936.	1188.	1531.
COMPOSITION OF FOREIGN TRADE						
EXPORTS:						
CMEA	0.484	0.475	0.472	0.464	0.468	0.467
OTHER SOCIALIST	0.114	0.111	0.110	0.111	0.111	0.111
DEVELOPED WEST	0.248	0.280	0.285	0.290	0.286	0.288
DEVELOPING COUNTRIES	0.096	0.102	0.102	0.103	0.103	0.103
UNSPECIFIED	0.057	0.032	0.031	0.032	0.032	0.032
IMPORTS:						
CMEA	0.424	0.431	0.447	0.452	0.462	0.465
OTHER SOCIALIST	0.100	0.100	0.105	0.107	0.107	0.106
DEVELOPED WEST	0.359	0.365	0.338	0.329	0.319	0.316
DEVELOPING COUNTRIES	0.117	0.104	0.109	0.112	0.112	0.113

SRI-WEFA ECONOMETRIC MODEL OF THE SOVIET UNION
BASELINE FOR CFR STUDY (11/9/77)

TABLE 5.00 FOREIGN TRADE

foreign trade continued

GROWTH OF FOREIGN TRADE

ITEM	1975	1976	1977	1978	1979	1980
EXPORTS TO:						
CMEA-------	43.16	11.71	10.46	7.08	10.61	9.41
OTHER SOCIALIST----	19.87	10.63	10.81	10.09	9.59	9.21
DEVELOPED WEST-----	0.11	28.61	13.07	10.86	8.20	10.38
DEVELOPING COUNTRIES-----	16.02	21.87	10.50	10.14	9.83	9.56
UNSPECIFIED-------	-6.67	-36.97	10.00	10.00	9.99	9.00
TOTAL EXPORTS---------	21.11	13.96	11.22	8.89	9.70	9.67
IMPORTS FROM:						
CMEA------	38.03	9.09	9.89	9.35	12.21	10.01
OTHER SOCIALIST----	65.26	7.50	11.08	10.17	9.45	8.87
DEVELOPED WEST------	66.27	9.17	-1.95	5.23	6.51	8.02
DEVELOPING COUNTRIES-----	30.89	-4.45	11.37	10.52	10.07	9.88
TOTAL IMPORTS---------	48.59	7.38	5.84	8.17	9.80	9.24

SRI-WEFA ECONOMETRIC MODEL OF THE SOVIET UNION
BASELINE FOR CFR STUDY (11/9/77)

TABLE 5.00 FOREIGN TRADE

ITEM	1980	1981	1982	1983	1984	1985
TOTAL EXPORTS,M,$US---	55024,	59924,	65419,	71140,	78302,	85498,
-GROWTH--	9.67	8.91	9.17	8.74	10.07	9.19
TOTAL IMPORTS,M,$US---	54471,	60158,	64772,	70849,	77607,	85084,
-GROWTH--	9.24	10.44	7.67	9.38	9.54	9.64
TOTAL NET EXPORTS,M$US	552,	-234,	648,	290,	695,	411,
CMEA, M,US$						
EXPORTS,TOTAL---	25671,	28074,	30353,	33265,	36846,	40045,
RAW MATERIALS---	15284,	16759,	18244,	20005,	21991,	24150,
MACHINERY---	6564,	7193,	7595,	8556,	9511,	10478,
GRAIN---	277,	272,	272,	273,	274,	274,
CONSUMPTION GOODS---	507,	528,	566,	588,	622,	647,
UNSPECIFIED---	3038,	3342,	3676,	4044,	4448,	4893,
IMPORTS,TOTAL---	25356,	27885,	30038,	32939,	36612,	40094,
RAW MATERIALS---	3556,	4115,	4673,	5297,	6018,	6762,
MACHINERY---	11648,	12721,	13419,	14714,	16663,	18302,
FOOD---	1258,	1350,	1436,	1533,	1627,	1735,
CONSUMPTION GOODS---	5065,	5602,	6127,	6704,	7285,	7927,
UNSPECIFIED---	3829,	4097,	4384,	4691,	5019,	5570,
NET EXPORTS---	337,	469,	339,	598,	257,	376,
OTHER SOCIALIST COUNTRIES,M,$US						
EXPORTS,TOTAL---	6100,	6694,	7356,	8078,	8856,	9687,
IMPORTS,TOTAL---	5787,	6455,	7111,	7799,	8515,	9259,
NET EXPORTS---	312,	239,	245,	280,	341,	428,

86

SRI-WEFA ECONOMETRIC MODEL OF THE SOVIET UNION
BASELINE FOR CFR STUDY (11/9/77)

TABLE 5.00 FOREIGN TRADE

ITEM	1980	1981	1982	1983	1984	1985
DEVELOPED WEST, M.$US						
EXPORTS,TOTAL	15852,	17070,	18890,	20189,	22143,	23999,
MACHINERY	977,	1076,	1234,	1326,	1484,	1620,
FUELS	8579,	9136,	10179,	10708,	11770,	12696,
OTHER MATERIALS	3079,	3378,	3728,	4130,	4584,	5089,
GRAIN	0,	0,	0,	0,	0,	0,
OTHER FOOD	318,	337,	357,	378,	399,	421,
MFG, CONSUMER GOODS	2899,	3143,	3391,	3646,	3906,	4172,
IMPORTS,TOTAL	17192,	19076,	20310,	22235,	24021,	26654,
MACHINERY	5743,	6371,	6737,	7412,	8020,	8970,
RAW MATERIALS	7336,	8261,	8873,	9782,	10648,	11935,
GRAIN	1248,	1273,	1299,	1325,	1351,	1378,
CONSUMER GOODS	1852,	2128,	2327,	2610,	2861,	3197,
UNSPECIFIED	1013,	1043,	1075,	1107,	1140,	1174,
NET EXPORTS	-1326,	-1608,	-1404,	-1558,	-1861,	-2636,

foreign trade continued

SRI-WEFA ECONOMETRIC MODEL OF THE SOVIET UNION
BASELINE FOR CFR STUDY (11/9/77)

TABLE 5.00 FOREIGN TRADE

I T E M	1980	1981	1982	1983	1984	1985
DEVELOPING COUNTRIES,M,$US						
EXPORTS,TOTAL	5661.	6189.	6753.	7356.	8000.	8688.
IMPORTS,TOTAL	6136.	6742.	7313.	7877.	8458.	9078.
NET EXPORTS	-474.	-553.	-560.	-521.	-458.	-390.
UNSPECIFIED EXPORTS,WORLD,M,$US	1741.	1897.	2068.	2254.	2457.	2678.
MACHINERY IMPORTS						
MACH. & EQUIP.,CHEMICAL, WEST,M,$US	747.	925.	1358.	1561.	1078.	1358.
MACHINERY, METAL WORKING, TOTAL,M,C,RB	1581.	1799.	1958.	2206.	2456.	2812.
MACHINERY, MINING, MET,&PETROL,, TOTAL,M,C,RB	1331.	1499.	1439.	1608.	2040.	2295.
COMPOSITION OF FOREIGN TRADE						
EXPORTS:						
CMEA	0.467	0.468	0.464	0.468	0.471	0.473
OTHER SOCIALIST	0.111	0.112	0.112	0.114	0.113	0.113
DEVELOPED WEST	0.288	0.285	0.289	0.284	0.283	0.291
DEVELOPING COUNTRIES	0.103	0.103	0.103	0.103	0.102	0.102
UNSPECIFIED	0.032	0.032	0.032	0.032	0.031	0.031
IMPORTS:						
CMEA	0.465	0.464	0.464	0.465	0.472	0.471
OTHER SOCIALIST	0.106	0.107	0.110	0.110	0.110	0.109
DEVELOPED WEST	0.316	0.317	0.314	0.314	0.310	0.313
DEVELOPING COUNTRIES	0.113	0.112	0.113	0.111	0.109	0.107

SRI-WEFA ECONOMETRIC MODEL OF THE SOVIET UNION
BASELINE FOR CFR STUDY (11/9/77)

TABLE 5.00 FOREIGN TRADE

foreign trade continued

I T E M	1980	1981	1982	1983	1984	1985
GROWTH OF FOREIGN TRADE						
EXPORTS TO:						
CMEA	9.41	9.36	8.12	9.59	10.77	9.76
OTHER SOCIALIST	9.21	9.74	9.89	9.82	9.63	9.39
DEVELOPED WEST	10.58	7.69	10.66	6.88	9.68	8.38
DEVELOPING COUNTRIES	9.56	9.32	9.11	8.92	8.76	8.61
UNSPECIFIED	9.00	9.00	9.00	9.00	9.00	9.00
TOTAL EXPORTS	9.67	8.91	9.17	8.74	10.07	9.19
IMPORTS FROM:						
CMEA	10.01	9.97	7.72	9.66	11.15	9.51
OTHER SOCIALIST	8.87	11.54	10.16	9.68	9.19	8.73
DEVELOPED WEST	8.02	10.96	6.47	9.48	8.03	10.96
DEVELOPING COUNTRIES	9.88	9.88	8.47	7.71	7.37	7.33
TOTAL IMPORTS	9.24	10.44	7.67	9.38	9.54	9.64

SRI-WEFA ECONOMETRIC MODEL OF THE SOVIET UNION
BASELINE FOR CFR STUDY (11/9/77)

TABLE   6.00 TRADE & HARD CURRENCY BALANCES

I T E M	1975	1976	1977	1978	1979	1980
SOVIET TRADE BALANCE WITH:						
CMEA----	586.00,	902.15,	1043.41,	692.52,	648.66,	336.71
-IMPORT/EXPORT RATIO---	0.98,	0.95,	0.95,	0.97,	0.98,	0.99
OTHER SOCIALIST---	84.,	209.,	220.,	239.,	269.,	312.,
-IMPORT/EXPORT RATIO---	0.98,	0.95,	0.95,	0.95,	0.95,	0.95,
DEVELOPED WEST---	-5034.42,	-3852.75,	-2216.18,	-1655.95,	-1251.23,	-1325.86
-IMPORT/EXPORT RATIO---	1.61,	1.37,	1.19,	1.13,	1.11,	1.08
DEVELOPING COUNTRIES---	-1142.,	-256.,	-319.,	-369.,	-417.,	-474.
-IMPORT/EXPORT RATIO---	1.36,	1.07,	1.07,	1.08,	1.08,	1.08
HARD CURRENCY BALANCES,M,$US						
INFLOWS						
NET BALANCE OF TRADE---	-6281.,	-4315.,	-2825.,	-2285.,	-1884.,	-2025.,
NET BAL. OF SERVICES & TRNSFRS	200.,	300.,	330.,	363.,	599.,	439.,
CREDIT DRAWINGS---	4300.,	4450.,	4200.,	4500.,	4800.,	5100.,
GOLD SALES---	1000.,	1250.,	1500.,	1600.,	1700.,	1800.,
OUTFLOWS						
INTEREST PAYMENTS---	276.,	500.,	698.,	871.,	1024.,	1161.,
CREDIT REPAYMENTS---	1272.,	1903.,	2040.,	2681.,	3236.,	3728.,
NET INFLOWS---	-2329.,	-719.,	467.,	625.,	755.,	426.,
HARD CURRENCY HOLDINGS,M,$US---	-1594.,	-2313.,	-1846.,	-1220.,	-465.,	-39.,
DEBT OUTSTANDING,M,$US---	7489.,	10036.,	12196.,	14015.,	15579.,	16951.,
DEBT MINUS HARD CURRENCY---	9083.,	12349.,	14041.,	15235.,	16044.,	16990.,

SRI-WEFA ECONOMETRIC MODEL OF THE SOVIET UNION
BASELINE FOR CFR STUDY (11/9/77)

TABLE 6.00 TRADE & HARD CURRENCY BALANCES

I T E M	1975	1976	1977	1978	1979	1980
GOLD RESERVES,TONS----------	1901.	1917.	1927.	1939.	1954.	1974.
-GOLD PRODUCTION,TONS-------	308.	330.	343.	357.	371.	386.
-GOLD SALES,TONS------------	190.	314.	333.	345.	356.	366.
-PRICE OF GOLD,M$US/TON-----	5.261	5.98	4.50	4.63	4.77	4.92
-PRICE OF GOLD,$US/OZ,------	163.70	123.79	139.97	144.16	148.49	152.94
GOLD RESERVES-IMPORT RATIO---	0.7541	0.5268	0.6106	0.6013	0.5860	0.5645
DEBT-EXPORT RATIO*-----------	1.1033	1.1663	1.1728	1.1478	1.1171	1.0718
DEBT SERVICE RATIO**---------	0.1880	0.2270	0.2287	0.2676	0.2966	0.3084

SRI-WEFA ECONOMETRIC MODEL OF THE SOVIET UNION
HASELINE FOR CFR STUDY (11/9/77)

TABLE   6.00 TRADE & HARD CURRENCY BALANCES

I T E M	1980	1981	1982	1983	1984	1985
SOVIET TRADE BALANCE WITH:						
CMEA	336,711	469,01	338,81	598,22	257,33	375,64
-IMPORT/EXPORT RATIO	0,99	0,99	0,99	0,99	0,99	0,99
OTHER SOCIALIST	312,	239,	245,	280,	341,	428,
-IMPORT/EXPORT RATIO	0,95	0,96	0,97	0,97	0,96	0,96
DEVELOPED WEST	-1325,86	-1607,55	-1404,11	-1557,94	-1860,75	-2635,55
-IMPORT/EXPORT RATIO	1,08	1,12	1,08	1,10	1,08	1,11
DEVELOPING COUNTRIES	-474,	-553,	-560,	-521,	-458,	-590,
-IMPORT/EXPORT RATIO	1,08	1,09	1,08	1,07	1,06	1,04
HARD CURRENCY BALANCES, M,$US						
INFLOWS						
NET BALANCE OF TRADE	-2025,	-2380,	-2206,	-2295,	-2485,	-3093,
NET BAL. OF SERVICES & TRNSFRS	439,	483,	531,	585,	643,	707,
CREDIT DRAWINGS	5100,	5400,	5700,	6000,	6300,	6600,
GOLD SALES	1800,	1944,	2100,	2267,	2449,	2645,
OUTFLOWS						
INTEREST PAYMENTS	1161,	1285,	1401,	1511,	1615,	1716,
CREDIT REPAYMENTS	3728,	4171,	4579,	4959,	5320,	5665,
NET INFLOWS	426,	-9,	145,	87,	-28,	-522,
HARD CURRENCY HOLDINGS, M,$US	-39,	-48,	96,	184,	155,	-367,
DEBT OUTSTANDING, M,$US	16951,	18180,	19301,	20342,	21322,	22257,
DEBT MINUS HARD CURRENCY	16990,	18228,	19205,	20158,	21167,	22624,

92

SRI-WEFA ECONOMETRIC MODEL OF THE SOVIET UNION
BASELINE FOR CFR STUDY (11/9/77)

TABLE 6.00 TRADE & HARD CURRENCY BALANCES

I T E M	1980	1981	1982	1983	1984	1985
GOLD RESERVES,TONS-----------	1974.	1991.	2006.	2019.	2028.	2034.
-GOLD PRODUCTION,TONS--------	366.	401.	418.	434.	452.	470.
-GOLD SALES,TONS-------------	366.	384.	402.	422.	442.	464.
-PRICE OF GOLD,M$US/TON------	4.92	5.06	5.22	5.37	5.53	5.70
-PRICE OF GOLD,$US/OZ,-------	152.94	157.53	162.26	167.13	172.14	177.30
GOLD RESERVES-IMPORT RATIO---	0.5645	0.5287	0.5153	0.4878	0.4672	0.4349
DEBT-EXPORT RATIO-----------	1.0718	1.0678	1.0167	0.9985	0.9559	0.9427
DEBT SERVICE RATIO*---------	0.3084	0.3197	0.3166	0.3205	0.3132	0.3076

93

SRI-WEFA ECONOMETRIC MODEL OF THE SOVIET UNION
BASELINE FOR CFR STUDY (11/9/77)

TABLE 12.00 KEY ASSUMPTIONS

ITEM	1975	1976	1977	1978	1979	1980
DEMOGRAPHIC (MILLIONS OF PERSONS)						
TOTAL POPULATION	255.500	257.900	260.400	263.150	265.750	268.590
-GROWTH	0.87	0.94	0.97	1.06	0.99	0.99
ABLE BODIED POPULATION	144.410	147.200	149.880	152.230	154.190	155.770
-GROWTH	1.19	1.93	1.82	1.57	1.29	1.02
WEATHER (DEVIATION FROM NORMAL)						
SPRING-SUMMER PRECIPITATION	-0.111	0.0	0.0	0.0	0.0	0.0
WINTER PRECIPITATION	-0.58	0.0	0.0	0.0	0.0	0.0
WINTER TEMPERATURE	-0.08	0.0	0.0	0.0	0.0	0.0
DEFENSE (H.CURR & M. OF PERSONS)						
STATE BUDGET EXPENDITURES	17.400	17.200	17.200	17.888	18.604	19.348
-GROWTH	-1.69	-1.15	0.0	4.00	4.00	4.00
NON-PERSONNEL OPERATING EXPENDITURES	8.700	8.700	9.048	9.410	9.786	10.178
-GROWTH	-6.45	0.0	4.00	4.00	4.00	4.00
DEFENSE PROCUREMENT	15.600	16.200	16.848	17.522	18.223	18.952
-GROWTH	10.64	3.85	4.00	4.00	4.00	4.00
RESEARCH & DEVELOPMENT	8.800	9.150	9.516	9.897	10.293	10.704
-GROWTH	7.32	3.98	4.00	4.00	4.00	4.00
MILITARY MANPOWER	4.005	4.010	4.010	4.010	4.010	4.010
-GROWTH	4.43	0.12	0.0	0.0	0.0	0.0
PLANNED ACCUMULATION (% GROWTH)						
CENTRALIZED INVESTMENT	8.001	4.00	4.00	4.00	4.00	4.00
TRANSPORT/COMM. FINANCING	6.821	4.26	5.00	5.00	5.00	4.50
AGRICULTURE FINANCING	13.461	4.31	5.68	5.00	5.00	5.00

94

SRI-WEFA ECONOMETRIC MODEL OF THE SOVIET UNION
BASELINE FOR CFR STUDY (11/9/77)

TABLE 12.00 KEY ASSUMPTIONS

ITEM	1975	1976	1977	1978	1979	1980
WORLD TRADE PRICES (% GROWTH)						
OFFICIAL SOVIET IMPORT PRICE INDEX---	19.68	5.86	4.00	4.00	4.00	4.00
OFFICIAL SOVIET EXPORT PRICE INDEX---	12.82	4.60	5.00	5.00	5.00	5.00
WORLD MARKET PRICE OF GRAIN---	-8.21	8.94	2.00	2.00	2.00	2.00
WORLD GOLD PRICE---	13.82	-24.38	15.07	3.00	3.00	3.00
U.S. RAW MATERIALS IMPORT PRICES---	4.50	7.69	7.92	5.69	3.00	6.11
GERMAN NON-ELECT. MACH. EXPORT PR, ---	9.80	7.64	7.00	7.00	6.50	6.00
U.S. FUEL IMPORT PRICES---	1.16	6.83	7.13	7.14	7.00	7.00
RATIO OF SOVIET FUEL TO						
RAW MATERIAL EXPORT PRICES---	1.41	1.40	1.42	1.44	1.47	1.49
PRICE OF IMPORTS FROM THE OW OF:						
MACHINERY---	9.83	6.19	6.00	6.00	6.00	6.00
RAW MATERIALS & FUELS---	-5.50	6.98	7.00	7.00	7.00	7.00
FOOD PRODUCTS---	2.90	4.17	4.00	4.00	4.00	4.00
INDUSTRIAL CONSUMER GOODS---	3.75	4.28	4.00	4.00	4.00	4.00
PRICE OF IMPORTS FROM CMEA COUNTRIES:						
MACHINERY---	9.57	4.06	4.00	4.00	4.00	4.00
RAW MATERIALS & FUELS---	8.78	5.22	5.00	5.00	5.00	5.00
FOOD PRODUCTS---	13.07	1.88	2.00	2.00	2.00	2.00
INDUSTRIAL CONSUMER GOODS---	13.04	1.87	2.00	2.00	2.00	2.00
AGGREGATE INDEX---	12.29	3.45	3.00	3.00	3.00	3.00
PRICE OF EXPORTS TO CMEA COUNTRIES:						
MACHINERY---	0.56	11.61	4.00	4.00	4.00	4.00
RAW MATERIALS & FUELS---	38.20	5.00	5.00	5.00	5.00	5.00
FOOD PRODUCTS---	32.77	2.84	2.00	2.00	2.00	2.00
INDUSTRIAL CONSUMER GOODS---	6.98	2.36	2.00	2.00	2.00	2.00

SRI-WEFA ECONOMETRIC MODEL OF THE SOVIET UNION
BASELINE FOR CFR STUDY (11/9/77)

TABLE 12.00 KEY ASSUMPTIONS

I T E M	1975	1976	1977	1978	1979	1980
WORLD TRADE VARIABLES (% GROWTH)						
TOTAL IMPORTS OF DW	-1.72	8.42	6.80	7.27	7.00	6.50
TOTAL IMPORTS OF LDC-S	-1.33	7.16	7.00	7.00	7.00	7.00
DW IMPORTS OF FUEL & MATERIALS	-4.96	6.80	7.00	7.00	7.00	7.00
INDUSTRIAL PRODUCTION OF DW	-2.27	5.21	4.00	5.00	5.00	5.00
NET MATERIAL PRODUCT OF CMEA	6.06	3.81	6.50	6.50	6.50	6.50
HARD CURRENCY VARIABLES ($M)						
GRAIN IMPORTS FROM THE DW	1880.000	3000.000	1800.000	1200.000	1223.999	1248.479
-GROWTH	269.35	59.57	-40.00	-13.33	2.00	2.00
CREDIT DRAWINGS	4300.000	4450.000	4200.000	4500.000	4800.000	5100.000
-GROWTH	151.46	3.49	-5.62	7.14	6.67	6.25
GOLD SALES	1000.000	1250.000	1500.000	1600.000	1700.000	1800.000
-GROWTH	25.00	25.00	20.00	6.67	6.25	5.88
ASSUMED DEBT SERVICE RATIO TARGET	0.17	0.22	0.23	0.26	0.24	0.31

SRI-WEFA ECONOMETRIC MODEL OF THE SOVIET UNION
BASELINE FOR CFR STUDY (11/9/77)

TABLE 12.00 KEY ASSUMPTIONS

ITEM	1980	1981	1982	1983	1984	1985
DEMOGRAPHIC (MILLIONS OF PERSONS)						
TOTAL POPULATION	268.390	271.060	273.740	276.420	279.070	281.660
-GROWTH	0.99	0.99	0.99	0.98	0.96	0.93
ABLE BODIED POPULATION	155.770	156.930	157.730	158.290	158.770	159.190
-GROWTH	1.02	0.74	0.51	0.35	0.30	0.26
WEATHER (DEVIATION FROM NORMAL)						
SPRING-SUMMER PRECIPITATION	0.0	0.0	0.0	0.0	0.0	0.0
WINTER PRECIPITATION	0.0	0.0	0.0	0.0	0.0	0.0
WINTER TEMPERATURE	0.0	0.0	0.0	0.0	0.0	0.0
DEFENSE (B.CUR,R & M, OF PERSONS)						
STATE BUDGET EXPENDITURES	19.348	20.122	20.926	21.763	22.634	23.559
-GROWTH	4.00	4.00	4.00	4.00	4.00	4.00
NON-PERSONNEL OPERATING EXPENDITURES	10.178	10.585	11.008	11.449	11.907	12.383
-GROWTH	4.00	4.00	4.00	4.00	4.00	4.00
DEFENSE PROCUREMENT	18.952	19.710	20.498	21.318	22.171	23.058
-GROWTH	4.00	4.00	4.00	4.00	4.00	4.00
RESEARCH & DEVELOPMENT	10.704	11.132	11.578	12.041	12.522	13.023
-GROWTH	4.00	4.00	4.00	4.00	4.00	4.00
MILITARY MANPOWER	4.010	4.010	4.010	4.010	4.010	4.010
-GROWTH	0.0	0.0	0.0	0.0	0.0	0.0
PLANNED ACCUMULATION (% GROWTH)						
CENTRALIZED INVESTMENT	4.00	4.00	4.00	4.00	4.00	4.00
TRANSPORT/COMM. FINANCING	4.50	4.00	4.00	4.00	4.00	4.00
AGRICULTURE FINANCING	5.00	4.99	5.00	5.00	5.00	5.00

SRI-WEFA ECONOMETRIC MODEL OF THE SOVIET UNION
BASELINE FOR CFR STUDY (11/9/77)

TABLE 12.00 KEY ASSUMPTIONS

ITEM	1980	1981	1982	1983	1984	1985
WORLD TRADE PRICES (% GROWTH)						
OFFICIAL SOVIET IMPORT PRICE INDEX---	4.00	4.00	4.00	4.00	4.00	4.00
OFFICIAL SOVIET EXPORT PRICE INDEX---	5.00	4.00	4.00	4.00	4.00	4.00
WORLD MARKET PRICE OF GRAIN------	2.00	2.00	2.00	2.00	2.00	2.00
WORLD GOLD PRICE-----	3.00	3.00	3.00	3.00	3.00	3.00
U.S. RAW MATERIALS IMPORT PRICES---	6.11	5.75	5.44	5.16	4.91	4.68
GERMAN NON-ELECT. MACH. EXPORT PR.--	6.00	5.50	5.50	5.50	5.50	5.50
U.S. FUEL IMPORT PRICES-----	7.00	7.00	7.00	7.00	7.00	7.00
RATIO OF SOVIET FUEL TO						
RAW MATERIAL EXPORT PRICES-----	1.49	1.52	1.54	1.56	1.59	1.61
PRICE OF IMPORTS FROM THE DW OF:						
MACHINERY---------	6.00	5.50	5.50	5.50	5.50	5.50
RAW MATERIALS & FUELS------	7.00	7.00	7.00	7.00	7.00	7.00
FOOD PRODUCTS---------	4.00	4.00	4.00	4.00	4.00	4.00
INDUSTRIAL CONSUMER GOODS-----	4.00	4.00	4.00	4.00	4.00	4.00
PRICE OF IMPORTS FROM CMEA COUNTRIES:						
MACHINERY---------	4.00	4.00	4.00	4.00	4.00	4.00
RAW MATERIALS & FUELS------	5.00	5.00	5.00	5.00	5.00	5.00
FOOD PRODUCTS---------	2.00	2.00	2.00	2.00	2.00	2.00
INDUSTRIAL CONSUMER GOODS-----	2.00	2.00	2.00	2.00	2.00	2.00
AGGREGATE INDEX------	3.00	3.00	3.00	3.00	3.00	3.00
PRICE OF EXPORTS TO CMEA COUNTRIES:						
MACHINERY---------	4.00	4.00	4.00	4.00	4.00	4.00
RAW MATERIALS & FUELS------	5.00	5.00	5.00	5.00	5.00	5.00
FOOD PRODUCTS---------	2.00	2.00	2.00	2.00	2.00	2.00
INDUSTRIAL CONSUMER GOODS-----	2.00	2.00	2.00	2.00	2.00	2.00

SRI-WEFA ECONOMETRIC MODEL OF THE SOVIET UNION
HASELINE FOR CFR STUDY (11/9/77)

TABLE 12.00 KEY ASSUMPTIONS

ITEM	1980	1981	1982	1983	1984	1985
WORLD TRADE VARIABLES (% GROWTH)						
TOTAL IMPORTS OF DW----------------	6.50	6.00	6.00	6.00	6.00	6.00
TOTAL IMPORTS OF LDC-S-------------	7.00	7.00	7.00	7.00	7.00	7.00
DW IMPORTS OF FUEL & MATERIALS-----	7.00	7.00	7.00	7.00	7.00	7.00
INDUSTRIAL PRODUCTION OF DW--------	5.00	5.00	5.00	5.00	5.00	5.00
NET MATERIAL PRODUCT OF CMEA-------	6.50	6.25	6.00	6.00	6.00	6.00
HARD CURRENCY VARIABLES ($M)						
GRAIN IMPORTS FROM THE DW----------	1248,479	1273,447	1298,916	1324,893	1351,390	1378,417
-GROWTH----------------------------	2.00	2.00	2.00	2.00	2.00	2.00
CREDIT DRAWINGS--------------------	5100,000	5400,000	5700,000	6000,000	6300,000	6600,000
-GROWTH----------------------------	6.25	5.88	5.56	5.26	5.00	4.76
GOLD SALES-------------------------	1800,000	1944,000	2099,520	2267,480	2448,880	2644,790
-GROWTH----------------------------	5.88	8.00	8.00	8.00	8.00	8.00
ASSUMED DEBT SERVICE RATIO TARGET---	0.31	0.31	0.31	0.31	0.31	0.31

99

4

THE OUTLOOK FOR SOVIET AGRICULTURE

Barbara S. Severin and David W. Carey
Central Intelligence Agency

INTRODUCTION

Among industrialized nations, the Soviet Union is unique in its preoccupation with agriculture. Agriculture accounts for roughly one-fifth of the USSR's gross national product, employs one-quarter of its labor force, absorbs slightly more than one-quarter of its investment funds, yet is a perennial problem. Supply of and demand for key agricultural products are in disequilibrium more often than not. Harvest shortfalls, if not disasters, occur regularly, and the effects last months -- sometimes years.

The problem does not arise from neglect, at least not neglect since the mid-1960's. The current regime has had a long and well-documented commitment to agriculture. Soon after the Brezhnev-Kosygin leadership came to power in 1964, it introduced an ambitious program to revamp the agricultural sector through increased investment and stepped-up deliveries of industrial materials and equipment. The program was designed to transform agriculture from an inefficient, labor-intensive, mainly crop-producing sector to an efficient, capital-intensive, multi-product sector, thereby reducing the instability in year-to-year production and providing reliable supplies of major farm products. Although growth in investment and in the flow of industrially produced materials such as fertilizer, lubricants, and electric power has not always reached planned targets, the resources allocated to agriculture have been massive and impressive. The farm sector has responded with dramatic increases in production of grain, meat, and other commodities.

Still the imbalance between supply and demand has persisted. Farm output has not kept pace with a demand stimulated by rapidly growing incomes as well as promises of dietary improvement. Production of the major farm crop --

grain -- fell short of demand in 6 of the past 13 years. Moreover, fluctuations in farm output have not been dampened, and harvest shortfalls have, on occasion, been severe enough to slow economic development, contribute to large foreign currency deficits, and jeopardize gains made in improving consumer diets.

Even though the basic problems are long-standing, several factors are converging to intensify the need for substantial progress. First, the expansion of meat supplies has been a key plank in the Brezhnev-Kosygin consumer program. The harvest disaster in 1975 dealt a severe blow to the livestock program. Momentum in this area must be regenerated rapidly. Second, with the prospect that the supply of essential resources -- especially manpower -- will be increasingly tight, the Soviet economy can no longer afford a lagging sector that employs one out of every four workers. This plus mounting subsidies requires rapid gains in efficiency. Finally, evidence suggests that a considerable part of the gains made over the last decade were the result of unusually favorable weather and that this trend will not continue. If Soviet weather is now returning to the harsher conditions that prevailed earlier, an added burden is placed on current efforts to transform agriculture.

Brezhnev's agricultural strategy for growth, stability, and efficiency is centered on land reclamation, fertilizer and other soil additives, and farm machinery and equipment. The strategy will support moderate increases in production but will also make farm products increasingly expensive. The present regime seems willing to pay the price. But their efforts will not significantly reduce the farm sector's vulnerability to the weather or lessen the need for foreign grain to ensure adequate supplies of meat. Even if a successor regime proves willing to maintain these costly policies, the basic difficulties of fluctuating weather imposed on an underlying domestic shortage of grain will persist.

The following discussion will review the Tenth Five Year Plan (1976-80) for agriculture and take account of progress achieved in the past two years. We then discuss factors likely to influence agricultural prospects for the remainder of the 1970s and the first half of the 1980s. Given these prospects, we examine the probable consequences for the consumer and for agricultural trade.

THE 1976-80 PLAN(1)

The directives in the Tenth Five Year Plan lay down specific goals for Soviet agriculture through 1980 and, barring massive reallocation of resources, suggest general guidelines for several years thereafter. No changes in the basic agricultural policies of the past decade are apparent. Specific output plans are generally consistent with or above long-term trends. Programs to provide more fertilizer, to increase the irrigated and drained area, and to build more grain storage are designed to dampen severe swings in production or to lessen the effects of yearly production fluctuations through maintenance of adequate reserves. Nevertheless, planned growth in the flow of resources to agriculture, although in keeping with the investment program for the rest of the economy, has been sharply reduced from the last Five Year Plan.

Production Goals

The value of net agricultural production is slated to grow at a rate of about 4 1/2 percent yearly during 1976-80; about 3 1/2 percent if average production for 1974-76 is substituted for the poor 1975 base year.(2) This rate exceeds the growth achieved during 1971-75 and is in large part predicated on plans for 1976-80 grain production to average 220 million tons, with a 1980 output of 235 million tons.

----

(1)

The bulk of the data used in this section was published in the original Tenth Five Year Plan, Pravda, 7 March 1976. A number of subsequent articles provided additional data and facilitated our analysis. See, for example, V. K. Mesyats in Vestnik sel'skokhozyaystvennoy nauki, No. 9, 1976, p. 1-10; N. Gusev in Ekonomika sel'skogo khozyaystva, No. 8, 1976, p. 14-26; G. Gaponenko in Planovoye khozyaystvo, No. 5, 1976, p. 28-39; and L. Bashchikov in Vestnik statistiki, No. 9, 1977, p. 3-11.

(2)

Net agricultural production is the estimated value of agricultural output in 1970 prices for sales and home consumption, including changes in inventories of livestock, less the value of farm products used for seed and livestock feed. For tabular material and a brief discussion of the methodology used to measure net agricultural production, see David W. Carey, "Soviet Agriculture: Recent Performance and Future Plans," in Soviet Economy in a New Perspective, U.S. Congress, Joint Economic Committee, October 1976, p. 575.

Actual output for the first two years -- a record 223.8 million tons in 1976 followed by 195.5 million tons in 1977 -- suggests that this goal will be difficult to reach.(3) Even if the 1980 target of 235 million tons is reached, production in 1978-79 would have to average roughly 218 million tons in order to fulfill the five-year plan. For reasons discussed below, four out of five consecutive years of grain production in excess of 200 million tons, a level exceeded only twice in Soviet history, is highly unlikely.

Other crops are also scheduled for marked increases (see Table 4.1). Production of cotton is to reach 9 million tons by 1980, a plan that undoubtedly will be met. Output of sugar beets -- which reached a record 99.9 million tons in 1976 -- is to average 95-98 million tons for the five years, a level consistent with projections based on a long-term trend. Goals for potatoes and sunflower seed, however, are less likely to be achieved; output of both fell short of their respective 1971-75 annual averages in 1976 and 1977. Although production of vegetables in 1976 exceeded the 1971-75 annual average, substantial increases will be needed if the plan goal is to be met.

Output targets for livestock products, particularly meat, were reduced in the wake of the distress slaughtering stemming from the short 1975 grain crop. Despite the 11 percent drop in meat output registered in 1976, it is still possible to reach planned average annual production for the five year period as well as the 1980 target of 17.3 million tons. Progress hinges on the grain supply. It is the use of grain for livestock feed that has sharply boosted the demand for grain and prolonged the supply-demand imbalance (see Figure 4.1). Since 1972 the Soviet leadership has demonstrated a willingness to support this program with foreign grain. Continued support will be needed. This underlies Soviet participation with the US in a long-term grain agreement, extending through 1980, which calls for the USSR to import a minimum of six million tons of US grain each year.

----

(3)
   The 1977 harvest figure was calculated from the average 1976-77 grain production figure of 209.6 million tons announced by N.K. Baybakov, Chairman of Gosplan, in December 1977 (Pravda, 15 December 1977). It is a slight upward revision of the 194 million ton figure released by Brezhnev on 2 November 1977.

TABLE 4.1
USSR: Selected Indicators Of Agricultural Production
(in Millions of Tons)

	1971-75 Average Annual	1976-80 Plan Average Annual	1976 Plan	1976 Actual	1977 Plan	1977 Actual	1978 Plan	1980 Plan
Grain	181.6	220	207	223.8	213	195.5	220	235
Cotton	7.7	8.5	NA	8.3	NA	8.7	8.5	9
Sugar Beets	76.0	95-98	94.7	99.9	95.6	93.3	96.2	NA
Potatoes	89.8	102	99.0	85.1	101.0	83.4	NA	104
Sunflower Seed	6.0	7.6	7.5	5.3	7.5	5.9	7.5	7.7
Vegetables	23.0	28.1	26.0	25.0	27.1	23.0	NA	30
Fruit and Berries	8.0	10.4	9.5	9.8	9.8	NA	NA	11.6
Grapes	4.4	6.5	5.5	5.4	5.9	NA	NA	NA
Meat	14.0	15-15.6	13.3	13.6	14.5	14.8	15.6	17.3
Milk	87.4	94-96	87.0	89.1	92.0	94.8	95.4	102
Eggs (billion)	51.4	58-61	53.0	55.6	58.2	61.0	62.6	66.8
Wool (thousand tons)	442	473	432	433	453	458	NA	515

Figure 4.1

USSR: GRAIN PRODUCTION AND UTILIZATION

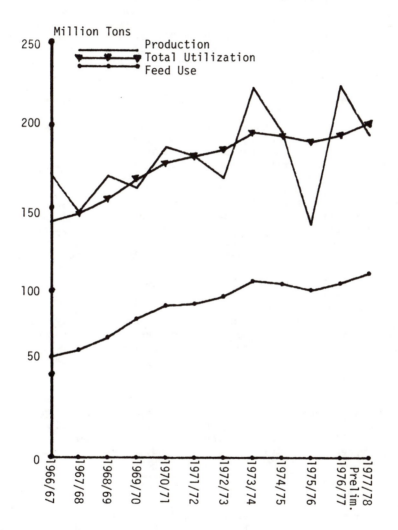

Input Plans

Agriculture will maintain its priority among resource claimants during the plan period. About one-fourth of new fixed investment in 1976-80 will go to agriculture, as it did during the past two plan periods. Yearly growth in the amount of funds channeled to agriculture will, however, be cut substantially. In keeping with a general tightening of investment funds throughout the economy, investment in agriculture is to grow at an average annual rate of only 3 1/2 percent, down sharply from the 9 1/2 percent recorded during 1971-75. Growth in the stock of plant and equipment will slow from the 11.3 percent yearly rate of 1971-75 to 8.4 percent during 1976-80.

Plans for the commitment of resources reflect the regime's continued concern with reducing fluctuations in production while increasing output. For example, programs to direct fertilizer and equipment to agriculture and to irrigate and drain additional cropland are designed to create zones of guaranteed agricultural production. In fact, fertilizer deliveries are the only inputs scheduled to continue increasing at past rates. By 1980, 120 million tons will be sent to farms, three-fifths more than the amount delivered in 1975. Fertilizer is probably the single most important yield-boosting factor. In addition, the area limed is to average 8 million to 10 million hectares yearly, compared to the 6 million hectares averaged during 1971-75. In contrast, planned shipments of tractors, trucks, and agricultural machinery will grow at sharply reduced rates. This slowdown in part reflects an industry approaching its output capacity with no evident plans for expansion. It also is consistent with the overall design for the economy; increases in productivity are to be an important source of growth. Combined inputs during 1976-80 are to grow 2.1 percent yearly with improvement in factor productivity(4) up 1.4 percent per year.

Land improvement will command a substantial portion of new fixed capital. Gross additions to irrigated land will amount to 4.9 million hectares and additions to drained land, 4.7 million hectares. The cost per hectare of land improvement has tripled since 1960 due primarily to increased

----

(4)
Growth of output not explained by growth of conventional inputs, that is, land, livestock, plant and equipment, current purchases (fertilizer, fuel, and others), and labor.

sophistication of the systems employed. Sprinkler systems are becoming more common, construction standards have been upgraded, and closed drainage systems are being emphasized. Although the initial costs are high, such improvements should help lower currently high retirement rates due to soil salinization. They will also lower water requirements per hectare.

The drive to stabilize farm output includes development of the Non-Black Soil Zone of the Russian Republic.(5) The zone is to receive an increased share of all types of inputs during 1976-80. For example, its share of gross fixed investment in agriculture will grow from nearly 15 percent during 1971-75 to just over 20 percent during 1976-80. Similarly, fertilizer deliveries to the zone will increase from 21 percent to 26 percent of total fertilizer deliveries. Delivery to agriculture of all types of equipment will grow faster in this area than in the rest of the country. Because the zone has the highest annual average rainfall of any large agricultural area of the European USSR, this concentration of resources could yield substantial production increases.

Immediate Prospects

In general, the plans for agricultural output during 1976-80 are internally consistent. For example, planned grain output -- if achieved -- would provide adequate supplies for food, industrial needs, and seed as well as for planned output of livestock products. Planned inputs also appear adequate to support planned output of most products -- with the key exceptions of vegetables and grain. Nevertheless, planned progress in agricultural development will depend on the interplay of the following: factor productivity, weather, labor supply, changing organizational structure, and availability of material inputs.

Factor Productivity. Soviet planners have identified productivity gains as the key to increasing agricultural production; 40 percent of the growth in farm output during

----

(5)
The Non-Black Soil Zone includes 29 oblasts, an area of about 52 million hectares in the northern European USSR. In 1975, this area produced 13 percent of the USSR's grain, 35 percent of its potatoes, 19 percent of its vegetables, 16 percent of its meat, and 21 percent of its milk. Grain production is scheduled to increase from 18.8 million tons in 1975 to 31 million tons in 1980. Other crops are to respond similarly.

107

1976-80 is to come from this source. This is only slightly better than the record for the past decade. About one-third of the increase in agricultural output during 1966-75 came from such intangibles as new technology, improved management, higher incentives, and the effect of weather, all of which improved productivity. There was, however, a striking difference between performance in the late 1960s and early 1970s. Almost two-thirds of the increase in production during 1966-70 was due to productivity gains, principally the result of increasingly good weather. In contrast, using three-year moving averages for net agricultural output, we find that 1971-75 was marked more by stability than growth; all the growth -- 6 percent -- in farm output was attributable to greater inputs, long relied on by Soviet planners to stimulate output. Indeed, the 10 percent growth in inputs during the period masked a 4 percent drop in factor productivity.

Falling productivity in the 1970s is partly accounted for by the nature of the input expansion. For example, changes in capital stock -- the gross value of buildings, machinery and equipment, and draft livestock -- are an important factor. Fixed capital grew about 8 1/2 percent per year in the late 1960s but increased almost 11 1/2 percent yearly during 1971-75. Presumably much of the construction is to support the regime's livestock program and is not immediately translated into increased production. According to some Soviet economists, the resulting increasingly negative return on capital will be reversed soon, as production catches up. In any event, productivity gains in Soviet agriculture are hard to obtain. A shift in weather for the worse could easily overshadow such gains and reduce growth to no more than that derived from increased inputs.

Weather. Weather is a key determinant of agricultural success.(6) Variations in weather have caused production to fluctuate sharply from year to year. For example, the grain crop in 1976, a year of favorable weather, was 60 percent larger than the drought-stricken 1975 crop. Between 1960 and 1976, however, there was a strong upward trend in grain production, amounting to almost an 80 percent increase, as a result of the use of more fertilizer and farm machinery, an 11

----

(6)
   Agriculture in the USSR faces severe environmental constraints. More than 20 percent of the country is too cold for agriculture, and an additional 40 percent is so cold that only hardy, early-maturing crops can be grown. Output of grain is handicapped by a short growing season and by insufficient moisture in many areas.

percent increase in sown area, the introduction of better seed varieties, a better crop mix, the improvement in planting and harvesting practices, and perhaps most important, improved climate during the period.(7) A comparison of the climate since 1960 with a long-term average shows that the stable period of increased moisture in the late 1960s and early 1970s in the steppe and near-desert regions was unusual. It also indicates that a steady improvement in the climate of the grain-growing region -- increased precipitation, warmer winters, cooler summers -- occurred between 1960 and 1970.(8) Continued improvement is unlikely because the amount of water the atmosphere can transport from the North Atlantic to the Soviet grain belt is physically limited. The dryness in 1975 combined with other global climate changes could have signaled the end to a period of dependable moisture in these areas and a return to the more "normal" conditions of the early 1960s, that is, years of nearly normal weather interspersed with years of above-normal and years of subnormal weather.(9)

Labor Supply. Available labor may constrain future agricultural output. Although farm workers still comprise over one-quarter of the total labor force, agricultural employment dropped from 45 million in 1960 to 34 million in 1976 as employment opportunities swelled in urban areas.(10) Mechanization offset much of the labor loss during the early 1960s, but by mid-decade, the leadership apparently felt the out-migration had to be slowed. A major program to reduce rural-urban wage differentials was instituted. Per capita money incomes of farm workers nearly doubled from 1965 to

----

(7)

Recent work indicates that over half the increase in grain production during 1962-74 was the result of improved climate. See CIA, Office of Economic Research Report, ER 76-10577, USSR: The Impact of Recent Climate Change on Grain Production, October 1976, p. 14.

(8)

See ibid. for a detailed discussion of possible changing climate.

(9)

"Above-normal" weather refers to conditions where crop loss caused by summer drought and cold winter temperatures is less than the long-run average. "Subnormal" weather produces greater-than-average losses.

(10)

Murray Feshbach and Stephen Rapawy, "Soviet Population and Manpower Trends and Policies" in Soviet Economy in a New Perspective, Joint Economic Committee, U.S. Congress, October 1976, p. 132.

1975.   Nevertheless,   average   farm   incomes   were roughly   30
percent lower than those of nonfarm workers in 1975.(11)

    Migration from farms involves primarily the young and the
more skilled, leaving behind people largely outside of working
age.   For example, almost half the rural population of 1970
was under 15 or over 59, compared with about one-third in
urban areas.   According to Soviet census data, between 1959
and 1970 the rural population in ages 20-34 declined by 33
percent while the urban population in those ages increased by
11 percent.   Available demographic data suggest the migration
may have   accelerated since   1970.(12) The   total rural
population, which declined from 109 million in 1959 to 106
million in 1970, fell further to 98 million by January 1977.
Although the urban birth rate is declining faster than the
rural, the overall decline and consequent slowdown in total
population growth is compounding the problem of out-migration.
Indeed, the decline in agricultural population, if continued,
could jeopardize farm output goals.

    The loss of trained personnel is having a more immediate
effect. Official statistics suggest that fewer than half the
graduates from agricultural institutions return to work on the
land. The leadership has stressed certain actions which may
eventually slow or even halt this decline.

        Agricultural   specialists,   who   had   been
    particularly   prone   to change   their   branch of
    employment, are to be controlled more closely in the
    future. Priority will be given to enrolling rural
    youth in agricultural studies, conditions for those
    assigned to work on farms are to be improved by the
    republic ministries of agriculture, and managers of
    individual farms are to be held strictly accountable
    for hiring only those with proper documents and not
    releasing young specialists without authority from
    their superiors.   The Ministry   of Agriculture
    U.S.S.R. and the Central Statistical Administration
    U.S.S.R. are enjoined to study the distribution and
    utilization of specialists and to determine what

                    ----

(11)
    Gertrude   Schroeder   and   Barbara   Severin,   "Soviet
    Consumption and Income Policies in Perspective," ibid., p.
    629.
(12)
    CIA, Office of Economic Research Report, ER 77-10012,
    USSR: Some Implications of Demographic Trends for
    Economic Policies, January 1977, p. 14.

other measures may be necessary to reduce labor turnover among this group.(13)

More recently, a November 1977 decree granted new incentives designed to increase the number of agricultural specialists at the farm working level.(14) The joint Party-government decree stressed that efficient agricultural production requires working level leadership by qualified specialists who understand both the technology and the economics of farming. It is aimed at bringing a large pool of agricultural specialists into direct responsibility for farm output. To make the shift attractive, farms can guarantee to pay the transferred specialists at their current level for up to two years. Other incentives include making living quarters available "on a priority basis" and providing the opportunity to purchase cars and motorcycles.

The labor pinch is being felt in other sectors of the economy as well, as shown in Philip Grossman's chapter. As this problem becomes more severe, it will become increasingly difficult to tolerate tying one-fourth of the labor force to agriculture. Policies to restrict the mobility of rural workers will either have to be officially relaxed, or as the pull of higher-paid urban jobs becomes stronger, migration to the cities will be unofficially tolerated.

Organizational Change. On the organizational front, the leadership has taken numerous steps over the past decade to encourage a more uniform system of farm management. This system includes continuing to move state and collective farms on convergent paths, blurring the distinctions between the two,(15) allowing the farm to choose its own basic unit of

----

(13)
     Feshbach and Rapawy, pp. 142-43.
(14)
     Pravda, 11 November 1977.
(15)
     The state farm is a state-run enterprise and, in the Soviet view, is the rural equivalent of an urban factory. The workers are state employees, and their wages are paid from state funds. The collective farm is nominally an autonomous peasants' cooperative financed from its own budget with the members sharing the profits. Major management decisions, however, are not made by individual farms but by the central or regional administrations. Recent policy has aimed at reducing the differences between the two. The move to self-financing by state farms, for example, was designed to make them more

labor organization -- the link (zveno) or the brigade(16) -- and stressing inter-farm cooperation. Specifically sanctioned are inter-kolkhoz, inter-sovkhoz, kolkhoz-sovkhoz, and agro-industrial associations.

These steps are aimed at increasing efficiency (mainly through the formation of larger units yielding economies of scale), facilitating the use of the latest scientific and technical achievements, and improving the quality of the labor force and capital stock. From an economic standpoint, these aims could be accomplished to a certain degree because they focus on real problems. For example, many farms on their own resources cannot afford the latest equipment, attract highly trained technicians, or obtain quality services such as equipment repair. The reforms are likely to be subverted to some extent by the lack of incentives for large successful farms to cooperate with their poorer neighbors. Moreover, the success of these schemes will be seriously limited by the failure to reform the rigid framework -- price structure, incentives, centralized planning -- that binds each farm. Bold, innovative decisions affecting farm management and organization are unlikely from an aging leadership. Nor is output likely to be substantially increased by such tinkering.

Production can be more immediately stimulated, not through large inter-farm organizations but by encouraging

----

interested in becoming profitable, as collective farms have always had to be. Higher, more stable earnings and a social insurance system for the collective farmer are designed to bring his status closer to that of the state farm worker.

(16)

The link is a small group of peasants assigned a section of land and machinery on a long-time basis with earnings dependent on production. The brigade is a larger group of peasants assigned only a specific task, e.g., tractor operation, with earnings based on piece work. The link versus brigade debate -- apparent since links were first authorized during World War II -- has aroused more violent emotions than almost any other agricultural controversy in Soviet history, possibly because the link is felt to foster private property instincts. Use of the link form has fluctuated as officials blew hot and cold. The renewed popularity of the link is apparent in Stavropol' Kray, where, in 1976, 84 percent of the sown area was to be handled by links. Nearly 60 percent of the 1500 links in operation had been organized in 1976. (Ekonomicheskaya gazeta, No. 20, 1976, p. 18.)

small private producers. About one-quarter of total agricultural output, including one-fifth of the crops and one-third of the livestock products, comes from the private sector. Private agricultural production is derived from small land holdings, averaging less than one-half hectare, frequently combined with one or two head of livestock and a small flock of poultry.

The long-run policy toward this sector has been constrictive, but restrictions have been temporarily relaxed after bad harvests. In the past, output in the private sector has been easily spurred by supplying more livestock and feed to individuals, lowering barriers to the use of public lands, and allowing some urban residents to own livestock. The current leadership has turned to the private sector in the past and is doing so again. An extensive campaign is underway, led by Brezhnev himself who said "it is too soon to curtail agricultural production on private subsidiary farms of kolkhozniks, workers and employees."(17) Local administrations are urged to "make full and active use of private plots." Farms are encouraged to sell young poultry and livestock to individuals and to make feed available. A paragraph in the new draft constitution affirms that citizens are permitted to have private farms within established limits.

Although stimulation of the private sector does afford an opportunity to increase agricultural production in the short run without direct state investment, there are some costs involved. Private farmers have access to areas in addition to their plots for livestock pasturing and to other resources such as feed, young livestock, farm tools, and other materials from farms. Without this assistance, the private sector could not play such an important role.

The impact of private producers, even in the short run, will be less than it has been in the past. There has been a distinct downward trend in share of output -- from 46 percent of total farm production in 1950 to 35 percent in 1960 and about 25 percent today. This trend will continue in keeping with the decline in rural population and possible increased demands on the individual worker's time as the on-farm labor force declines. In addition, growing farm incomes and the increasing availability of processed farm products make work in the private sector less attractive.

----

(17)
     Pravda, 26 October 1976.

Input Availability. The impact of planned inputs depends in large part on environmental and institutional factors. For example, moisture availability determines the effectiveness of fertilizer applications, and a reduction in the retirement rate for machinery can boost the stock of machinery beyond the level suggested by planned deliveries, while construction bottlenecks can counter the impact of planned irrigation projects. In concert, all of these factors play a major role in determining productivity increases.

Fertilizer -- By 1980, 120 million tons of fertilizer, including 5 million tons of feed additives, will be sent to farms, three-fifths more than the amount delivered in 1975. During 1976-80, fertilizer deliveries are the only inputs scheduled to continue to increase at past rates. Due to capacity constraints, much of this fertilizer will not be available immediately. Dozens of large, modern production facilities have to be finished to meet production targets. As a result, almost half of the fertilizer scheduled for the five-year period will be received during the last two years.

About one-third of the fertilizer delivered to farms in 1975 was applied to grain. By 1980, this amount will double. The impact of planned applications will be limited, however, by low quality,(18) improper chemical mix, excessive transportation and storage losses, and improper application.(19)

Two further factors will determine the effectiveness of additional fertilizer applications:

(1) Moisture -- As applications increase, the moisture required to secure full benefits also increases. Given the anticipated weather trend toward less dependable moisture, output gains from increased fertilizer applications may not reach planned levels.

----

(18)

The average nutrient content of fertilizer in 1975 was only 35 percent which means high transportation and application costs per nutrient unit. Moreover, granular fertilizers -- easier to apply than powders -- account for only 40 percent of fertilizer supplies.

(19)

For a more detailed examination of the likely impact of fertilizer on grain production during 1976-80, see CIA, Office of Economic Research Report, ER 77-10557, The Impact of Fertilizer on Soviet Grain Output, 1960-80, November 1977.

114

(2) Rate of application -- Gains from fertilizer do not follow an exponential curve. At some point, different for each crop, response rates will first slow, then decline. Indeed, excessive applications of fertilizer have been blamed for declining sugar beet yields in some areas. At the extreme, too much fertilizer may destroy the crop. The largest gains are achieved with the initial applications, as shown in the following tabulation based on the USSR's countrywide experience with grain:(20)

	Fertilizer Application	Response Rates
	(million tons)	(tons of grain per ton of fertilizer)
Before 1969	1 to 10	2 to 3
1969-73	up to 20	1.2 to 1.5
1974-75	up to 25	1.2 to 1.3

Machinery -- Negative effects from the previously noted slowdown in machinery deliveries may be offset by other factors. The stock of tractors is slated to reach 2.85 million in 1980, and a stock of 800,000 combines is targeted. These plans suggest lower retirement rates during 1976-80, allowing faster-than-normal expansion of stocks despite slower growth in deliveries. The trend to larger tractors with greater horsepower and the recent introduction of new combine models will mean qualitative improvements as well. At the same time, one high-power tractor out of commission because of poor repair or lack of spare parts may cause more disruption than several smaller incapacitated tractors. Improvements in the mix of farm equipment would increase the productive capacity of existing stocks, but the failure to produce complementary agricultural machinery for higher horsepower tractors has been a constant complaint for a decade. Failure to supply adequate spare parts for existing equipment --

----

(20)
   Ibid., p. 9.

115

another key to improved productivity -- is also an often heard complaint.(21)

Land reclamation -- Plans for land reclamation have been hindered by the familiar problems that affect all major construction projects in the USSR: excessive new starts -- which scatter available equipment and skilled personnel as well as tie-up capital in unfinished projects -- and poor quality control. The emphasis is on building new projects, not reconstructing old. Yet there is abundant evidence that reconstruction, particularly of irrigation systems, is badly needed. Some of the large irrigation systems in Central Asia, for example, are said to lose as much as 40 to 50 percent of their water through seepage and evaporation.

The scheduled improvements are most meaningful for the grain program. While much of the current stock of improved land is used for technical crops such as cotton, about 20 percent is used for grain production. Average grain yields in 1972-76 were three-quarters greater on irrigated land than on non-improved land. Moreover, year-to-year variation in yield on improved land is less. The Soviets expect to raise the grain yield on irrigated land to 35 centners per hectare by 1980, 5 centners more than in 1976. If plans are met, irrigated acreage would still represent a small share of the USSR's grain area but would produce 13 to 15 million tons, about 6 percent of the 1980 planned output of 235 million tons.

A growing lack of water may hamper development of new irrigation systems. Although hydropower plants are resisting reallocation of water to irrigation systems, as are fishing and other water-dependent enterprises,(22) recent power shortages in the Volga valley may have resulted partly from diversion of water to irrigation. The need for increased agricultural output, particularly of grain, hay, and pastures needed to support the livestock program, will have to be

----

(21)
The shortage of spare parts appears to be endemic. As recently as 1975, only 75 percent to 85 percent of the needed parts were available. Vestnik sel'sko-khozyaystvennoy nauki, No. 3, 1975, p. 30.
(22)
See Literaturnaya gazeta, 5 January 1977, p. 11, for an account of one such dispute.

balanced against the need for increased hydroelectric power.(23)

AFTER THE TENTH FIVE-YEAR PLAN

Decisions being made now are shaping the prospects for Soviet agriculture in the early 1980s. The Soviets will almost certainly continue programs that emphasize increased use of fertilizer, more machinery, and larger areas of irrigated and drained land. Even if a new regime attempts an infusion of greater inputs, capacity limitations in key industries such as fertilizer and agricultural machinery would delay deliveries. Increases in productivity are, therefore, the key, and these increases are determined mostly by the weather. Agricultural progress will be most easily measured by the output of grain and meat. The more meat production planned, the larger the requirement for grain. Although there is some hope that progress can be made in feeding efficiencies, there is only a slight chance that the USSR can solve its precarious position with regard to grain production and needs. If domestic production won't suffice, Moscow seems to have accepted the necessity to purchase foreign agricultural commodities to honor its program to improve diets. If the rest of the economy prospers and hard currency is available, this course of action will continue, but should foreign exchange become scarce, consumers will be asked, as they have often been asked in the past, to tighten their belts and do with less or no outside help. The widespread food shortages resulting from the 1975 harvest debacle confirmed that the USSR was prepared to impose at least limited hardships on its population when necessary.(24)

----

(23)

Potential oil shortages suggest thermal power plants will have to rely more on gas, coal, and nuclear sources. Availability of gas restricts potential gas-powered plants which are relatively simple to construct. Coal-powered plants are more difficult and take significantly more time to build. Massive nuclear plants are even further in the future. Thus, significant diversions of water from hydroelectric plants to irrigation would seem unlikely soon.

(24)

A negative hard currency trade balance may have been a factor in restraining Soviet grain imports during 1975-76. Grain imports of 26.4 million tons were high but not high enough to prevent distress slaughtering of hogs and poultry, the chief grain consumers. Hog numbers dropped from 72 million on 1 January 1975 to 58 million on 1

117

Availability of Inputs

Although investment programs are unlikely to change dramatically during the early 1980s, the agricultural sector will be affected by those problems that face the total economy -- a slowdown in the growth of capital investment and productivity, a sharp drop in the growth of the labor force, a bottleneck in steel output, and perhaps most crucial, a looming oil and hence energy shortage.

The current leadership recognizes the importance of a steady capital infusion into agriculture, but the projected slowdown in overall growth of the economy in the 1980s precludes investment growth in agriculture at rates registered in the past. Competing needs for ever-scarcer investment resources may constrain the amounts that can be allocated to the agricultural sector more severely than the planned slowdown in growth suggests. It is conceivable, for example, that investment directly into agriculture and such areas basic to agriculture as fertilizer and farm machinery production will have to be postponed as the regime concentrates on developing new supplies of oil and other energy sources.

Furthermore, in recent years leaders have frequently voiced the need to obtain a proper return on additional agricultural investment. At the Central Committee plenum in October 1976, Brezhnev noted that "it was not easy to find" the funds earmarked for agriculture in this five-year plan and that "we had to curtail some of the requirements of other branches of the economy."(25) Morever, both the size and use of these funds have been questioned. Soviet practice is critically compared to that of the US, where less investment produces a larger return and where resources are devoted more to fertilizer, breeding, and so forth, and less to buildings. If the critics are heard, a sharp change in the direction of investment may occur. As yet, there are no indications of such a shift.

Increased fertilizer application and emphasis on selected types of machinery and equipment may help boost output, but the large volume of inputs that has in the past led to substantial growth in output is no longer readily available.

January 1976 and poultry numbers from 792 million to 735 million (Central Statistical Administration, Narodnoye khozyaystvo SSSR v 1975 g., Moscow, 1976, pp. 391, 395).
(25)
Pravda, 26 October 1976.

For example, expansion of the land area now under cultivation
is unlikely; sown area in 1985 is planned at 218 million
hectares, the same as planned for 1980 and only fractionally
above the 1975 level.(26) The long-term decline in the
agricultural labor force will be compounded by a sharp drop in
the rate of growth of the total labor force in the 1980s (to
less than 1 percent yearly beginning in 1982). The resultant
demand from urban centers will make it increasingly difficult
to keep skilled workers on the farm.

Potential Output Levels

Specific production estimates for the 1980s cannot be
firm, but past trends, especially for important products such
as grain and meat, can be projected and examined. Grain
production since 1950 has grown 3.3 percent yearly(27) but has
been marked by sharp year to year fluctuations (see Figure
4.2). Continuation of this trend would leave the USSR about
15 million tons short of the 1980 goal of 235 million tons of
grain and suggests a 1985 crop of 245 million tons.(28)
Expectations regarding climate trends and the limited
contribution of technology during the next few years yield a
more conservative result. Grain production during 1976-80
would average around 200 million tons, 1980 output would be
about 213 million tons, and only in 1985 would production
reach 235 million tons.

Output of meat increased about 4 percent annually during
1951-77.(29) Continuation of this trend means that 1976-80
plans will barely be met and puts 1985 production at just over

----

(26)
Land reclamation efforts are continuing, but land
retirement, caused by long-term neglect or heavy usage,
has nearly offset new additions in recent years.
(27)
Calculated according to a formulation devised by Boris
Pesek. It closely resembles the least squares to log of
data method by taking the entire stream of values during
the period into account but has an additional constraint
-- the sums of the estimated trend values and of observed
values are equal. See Boris Pesek, "Economic Growth and
Its Measurement" in Economic Development and Cultural
Change, Volume IX, No. 3, April 1961, p. 295-303.
(28)
Corresponding calculations based on a 17 year trend
(1961-77) result in a 1985 output of 243 million tons.
(29)
Pesek formula.

Figure 4.2

USSR: GRAIN PRODUCTION

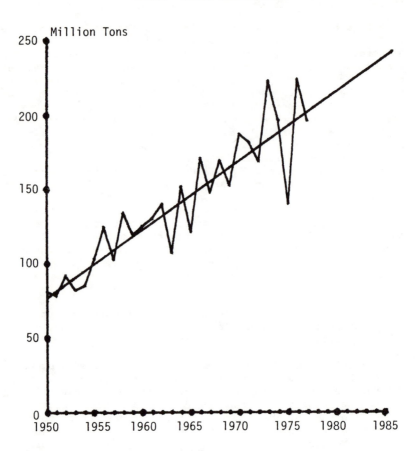

Million Tons

250

200

150

100

50

0

1950   1955   1960   1965   1970   1975   1980   1985

18 million tons.(30) Meat output over the past 26 years has not been subject to the wide year-to-year fluctuations experienced in grain production. In only 4 of the past 26 years has meat production declined from levels of the previous year. Because of the keen consumer interest in meat supplies, however, such declines are inordinately disruptive.

The USSR is attempting to increase meat production faster than the trend calculation suggests. An increasing share of productive investment is being directed to livestock complexes. Productivity statistics for these complexes for 1975 indicate much better performance than in the rest of the livestock sector, as shown in the following tabulation:

	USSR	Industrial Livestock Complexes
eggs per hen	200	220
pigs per sow	14	18
milk per cow (kg)	2,405	4,500

These complexes supplied 12 percent of the beef, 13 percent of the pork, and 20 percent of the poultry produced in that year. The share of output from these organizations is to almost double by 1980. If this goal is achieved and the trend toward industrialization continues, meat output could well exceed 18 million tons by 1985, requiring more grain than the

---

(30)
    If the trend is projected from 1951-75, 1985 production would be 18 1/2 million tons. Shortening the base period to 1961-76 puts 1985 production at 18 million tons.

USSR is likely to produce and further delaying a supply/demand equilibrium for grain.(31)

Some long-run adjustments in policies and practices could help to ease the pinch between grain supply and demand. Increased efficiency in the production of livestock products would be a major step forward but would depend on:

- the use of balanced feed rations, including greater use of mixed feed with protein supplements;

- the use of higher quality forage, requiring improvements in the production, preparation, and storage of hay, haylage, and silage;

- breed improvements, with concentration on beef cattle rather than on dual purpose animals; and

- refinement of the techniques needed to make large-scale livestock complexes successful.

If accomplished, these measures could push meat production in 1985 well above current projections. At the same time, the new-found feeding efficiencies would reduce the amount of grain required by the livestock sector, bringing total requirements more in line with likely grain production.

Rapid progress toward this goal is not likely. Typical of complaints is the following:

In a number of instances construction of livestock breeding complexes is carried out in isolation from the fattening base, the complexes are not being provided with highly productive cattle, and there is a lack of expeditious preparation of

----

(31)
If feeding rates are constant during the next decade, the 1985 estimated meat production of 18 million tons suggests a feed grain requirement of roughly 140 million tons. With other requirements -- seed, food, and industrial use -- projected at roughly 95 million tons, a harvest of 235 million tons -- exactly the crop projected above -- would be the minimum necessary to cover 1985 domestic requirements. No grain would be available for additions to stocks or exports. Should efforts to boost meat production more rapidly prove successful and, for example, 19 million tons be produced in 1985, a harvest of at least 245 million tons would be required.

122

worker personnel familiar with industrial technology. Here and there, in the name of specialization, there have been premature shutdowns of production of agricultural products on the usual commercial farms of the kolkhozes and sovkhozes. The Party Central Committee has decisively condemned such unwarranted actions and has ordered that the work of specialization and concentration of production be everywhere carried out in rational and economically correct fashion with due regard for overall state interests and local conditions of independent operation.(32)

Impact on the Consumer

The limited economic prospects for the next few years affect all aspects of consumer welfare, including diet. Slower economic growth over the next five to ten years means that the Soviet consumer will fare poorly in comparison to recent gains. Indeed, under projected economic growth rates, per capita consumption could grow no more than 2 percent a year in the early 1980s in contrast to about 3 1/2 percent since 1965. As a result, there will be no progress in closing the gap in living standards with the West or, for that matter, with most of Eastern Europe. Moreover, the combination of larger incomes over the next ten years and a slower growth in the availability of consumer goods will result in more widespread shortages and increasing consumer frustration.

A primary plank of the consumer program has been the promise to improve diets. Although real incomes have increased substantially over the past decade, the quality of the population's diet has not improved commensurately. The share of income spent for food has declined from 45 percent in the early 1960s to about 35 percent in 1975, but the Soviet people still obtain half of their daily calories from potatoes and grain products. Respectable gains have been made over the past decade in providing more quality foods -- especially meat -- but they seem only to have whetted the people's appetite for more. Consumers were particularly disappointed after the poor harvests of 1972 and 1975. Per capita food consumption dropped by a half percent following the 1972 harvest shortfall and fell by an unprecedented 3 percent in 1976 as the Soviet

----

(32)
Agitator, No. 18, September 1977, p. 19.

populace suffered from the worst food shortages in over a decade.(33)

At first glance, planners would appear to have recognized the difficulties inherent in achieving a stepped-up expansion in the supply of livestock products. The Tenth Five Year Plan emphasizes continued improvement in diet, but improvement derived primarily from increased consumption of fruits, vegetables, fish, and sugar, rather than from livestock products. There may be a stronger than anticipated reaction from the population. Plans for growth in incomes and in meat consumption imply an income elasticity of demand for meat of 0.2.(34) Soviet scholars estimate a range from 0.7 to 2.6, while Western experts postulate a 0.7 to 1.0 range.(35) If the true elasticity were 1.0, the discrepancy would amount to an unmet demand of 14 percent by 1980, a roughly 2 1/2 million ton shortage. The gap could well be larger; Soviet plans for income growth are consistently overfulfilled and, as economic growth slows, alternative outlets for discretionary income such as automobiles, furniture, and other major durables are

----

(33)

Following closely on the 1975 harvest failure there were numerous reports of widespread, prolonged shortages of many foods -- meat, dairy products, sugar, vegetables, and vegetable oil. Disappointment over sharply reduced meat supplies also reflected recollections of record consumption in 1975.

(34)

Per capita average income is planned to grow at about 3.2 percent per year while per capita meat consumption is scheduled to grow by 0.7 percent per year.

(35)

Part of the unusually high elasticity of demand for meat could reflect a desire for additional processing, better packaging, and other conveniences. Calculations for the United States over the period from 1909 to 1949-57 indicate an expenditure elasticity for all food of 0.77 which is a compound of an expenditure elasticity of 0.16 related to the demand for primary inputs of food as it leaves the farm gate and an expenditure elasticity of 1.62 for processing, transportation, and distribution costs. Simon Kuznets, "Quantitative Aspects of the Economic Growth of Nations," in Economic Development and Cultural Change, January 1962, Part II, p. 43. The evidence concerning the relative share of the primary inputs of food in retail prices in the USSR and the change in this share over time suggests that in the USSR the two elasticities are much closer together.

not likely to be expanded significantly. Thus, consumer frustration over meat shortages will continue well into the 1980s. A noted Soviet authority writing some years ago agreed, predicting that meat output would not reach demand until 1985-1990.(36)

The stubborn official policy of maintaining fixed retail prices in the face of rising disposable incomes, while pleasing to consumers, merely shifts a portion of agricultural production costs to the state while increasing the pressure on supplies of the more desired foods. For example, holding meat prices constant at the retail level set by Khrushchev in 1962,(37) cost the Brezhnev regime about 12 billion rubles in 1975. The total subsidy bill for agricultural products in 1975 was an estimated 17.2 billion rubles, equal to 15 percent of annual retail food purchases.(38) These expenditures are growing. During the Tenth Five Year Plan period the state budget has allocated 100 billion rubles to cover the difference between procurement costs for meat and milk and the prices paid by the consumer. "In these expenditures is found the real reflection of the politics of the Communist Party and the Soviet government directed at raising agricultural production and raising the material well-being of the Soviet population."(39)

Agricultural Trade

If production trends hold, consumer demand will have to be met at the margin with imported agricultural commodities. The USSR's foreign trade in agricultural products depends, of course, on the state of domestic supply and on the availability of hard currency. But recent experience indicates that the USSR is much more willing now to enter world markets than at any time in the past. Indeed, in 1975, the USSR ranked

----

(36)
    G. M. Loza, "Tekhnicheskiy progress i prognoz razvitiya sel'skogo khozyaystva na perspektivu," Vestnik selskokhozyaystvennoy nauki, No. 11, 1971, p. 3.
(37)
    In that year Khrushchev, citing the need to stimulate production of livestock products, increased prices of meat by an average 30 percent and of butter by 25 percent.
(38)
    Constance B. Krueger, "A Note on the Size of Subsidies on Soviet Government Purchases of Agricultural Products," ACES Bulletin, Vol. XVI, No. 2, Fall 1974, p. 66.
(39)
    Planovoye khozyaystvo, No. 7, 1977, p. 17.

as the world's fifth largest importer of agricultural commodities. Agricultural products in that year accounted for 25 percent of total USSR imports.(40)

In recent years, Soviet agricultural imports have centered on:

- Grain -- Net grain imports related to the 1975 crop shortfall amounted to roughly 22 million tons (see Figure 4.3). Almost all the imported grain came from hard currency countries.

- Raw sugar -- Raw sugar, traditionally from Cuba, accounted for one-quarter of the total value of agricultural imports in 1975. Moscow has also purchased substantial quantities of raw sugar from other countries such as Brazil, Australia, and the Philippines when poor sugar beet crops have coincided with short Cuban cane crops.

- Meat -- Imports reached record highs in 1974 and 1975, partly reflecting the program to improve diets but also in response to large world supplies and favorable prices (see Figure 4.4). The bulk of this trade consists of frozen meat -- mostly beef and mutton -- and poultry.

The USSR's major agricultural exports are:

- Cotton -- Since 1972, cotton has eclipsed grain as the primary export in three out of four years. This may be a regular occurence as the rising domestic demand for livestock feed and the fluctuation in grain output force a cutback in grain exports.

- Sunflower oil -- The USSR accounts for more than half of the world's exports of sunflower oil. Despite occasional domestic shortages of vegetable oil during the first half of the 1970s, sunflower oil exports remained fairly stable. Exports apparently were continued in order to take advantage of high world prices and to earn hard

----

(40)
All trade figures are based on official Soviet statistics as published in the annual foreign trade handbook. The most recent is Central Statistical Administration, Vneshnaya torgovlya SSSR v 1976 g., Moscow, 1977.

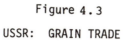

Figure 4.3

USSR: GRAIN TRADE

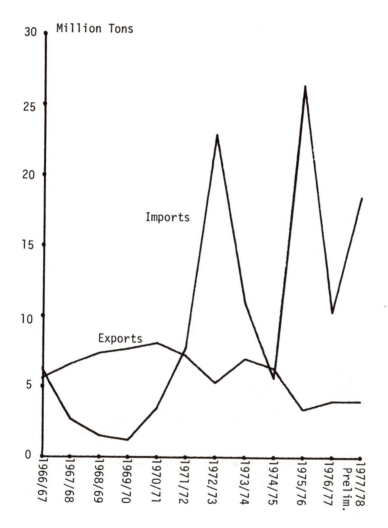

30 ⟋ Million Tons

25

20

Imports

15

Exports

10

5

0

1966/67
1967/68
1968/69
1969/70
1970/71
1971/72
1972/73
1973/74
1974/75
1975/76
1976/77
1977/78
Prelim.

Figure 4.4

USSR: MEAT TRADE

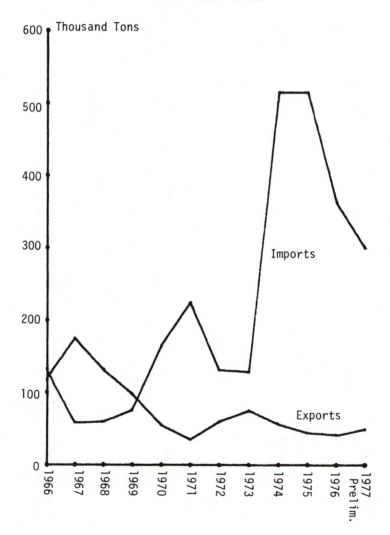

currency; about half the annual quantity exported goes to hard currency countries.

- Meat -- The USSR continues to export meat, a trade which seems contradictory to the regime's constant struggle to satisfy domestic demand. The bulk of these exports, however, go to Asian Communist countries and the less developed countries; this is probably viewed by the Soviets as a political-fraternal gesture. Most of the meat exported is canned and of relatively poor quality.

The USSR can be expected to remain a factor in world agricultural trade well into the 1980s, primarily as an importer. Substantial imports of grain will remain necessary unless the USSR experiences unexpectedly favorable weather. The only change in the pattern of grain imports between now and 1985 may be a greater stability in year-to-year purchases. Through 1980, the USSR has agreed to buy at least 6 million tons per year from the US. In the past, about half of yearly Soviet grain imports have been from the United States. To support a continued expansion of livestock inventories and meat production, we expect total imports of grain to vary between 10 million and 15 million tons in years of average crops and to rise to the 20 million to 25 million ton range after poor harvests. The USSR's influence on international grain markets extends beyond direct purchases. In lean years, Moscow has shown it can treat its traditional grain export clients roughly. With grain from the USSR no longer assured, Eastern Europe may emerge as a significant grain importer if hard currency is available.

Future Soviet meat imports are likely to be sporadic since the regime, while alert to bargain prices in the world market, seems to regard purchases as a last resort to support consumption levels. At no time has the USSR purchased quantities of meat in excess of 4 percent of annual consumption.

If Brezhnev's consumer policy is to be maintained, however, Moscow will have to resign itself to the fact that agricultural commodity trade will continue to exert a serious drag on the country's balance of payments, particularly with hard currency countries. In the 1970s the agricultural trade deficit with hard currency countries has been at least half of the total Soviet hard currency deficit. Moscow's ability to pay for agricultural commodity imports will be increasingly strained by the growing need for imports of Western machinery and technology and possibly oil as crude oil production slows. The regime's avowed dedication to the consumer will be severely tested, indeed perhaps proven, in the next decade.

WHAT'S AHEAD FOR SOVIET AGRICULTURE?

The future for Soviet agriculture looks very much like the past, plagued with problems. The problems that will face agriculture in the mid-1980s may be somewhat different from the problems faced today, but the results are likely to be the same. Agricultural production will not be sufficient to bring supply and demand to equilibrium, at least not for extended periods. As a result, some combination of disappointed consumers and continued dependence on imported agricultural supplies, notably grain, appears certain.

Our forecast of persisting hard times for agriculture is based largely on current investment strategy, likely weather patterns for the next several years, and the probable impact of an economy-wide tightening of the labor supply. The investment program on the books through 1980, which is likely to be matched by the program pursued thereafter, features a marked slowdown in the growth of inputs to agriculture. The program is in keeping with the economy-wide emphasis on increased efficiency in the use of available resources. However, the agricultural sector's record in achieving such efficiencies, and hence boosting productivity, is indeed spotty. The highpoints in agriculture's performance are attributable primarily to good weather, and weather will continue to be the dominant variable in Soviet agricultural production. Future weather conditions are never certain, of course, but as argued above it appears that the next ten years will not be as favorable as the last ten years. During the 1960s weather conditions were unusually favorable in the Soviet grain lands, especially when measured by the amount of precipitation. This trend is unlikely to continue because of physical limitations on the atmosphere's ability to transport water from the North Atlantic to the Soviet grain belt. Production will continue to fluctuate from year to year, and although bumper harvests can be expected, average production will fall below Soviet plans and requirements. An expected tightening in the economy's labor supply will also make productivity gains more difficult. Farm managers presently have difficulty in keeping younger, better-trained workers on the farm. As the demand for labor in urban industrial centers -- with higher real wages and better housing conditions -- increases, agriculture's position will deteriorate.

On the demand side, the leadership will be faced with continued growth in consumer demand for higher quality food, particularly meat. Over a decade ago, efforts to satisfy this demand launched the shift to a livestock economy. Such a shift sharply escalated the demand for grain and caused the

USSR to enter international grain markets as a major importer. Only by continuing the trend to large-scale livestock complexes can the Soviets hope to produce enough meat to mollify consumers. Such an emphasis, however, cuts two ways. It holds the promise of marked gains in production efficiency but requires a large and, more important, stable supply of grain. Once these complexes are operating, animals must be adequately maintained; as a result, the effects of harvest shortfalls, if not mitigated by imported grain, become more severe.

Soviet leaders have few alternatives during the next few years. There is little that can be done to alter the investment strategy which is largely designed to save labor; a larger share of investment funds for agriculture is unlikely as economic growth slows. Moreover, a transfer of resources within agriculture (for example, from construction of automated livestock feeders to expansion of capacity to produce traditional agricultural machinery) could boost grain output, but on balance would not save labor. Labor may well be the crucial factor in the 1980s. The alternatives may therefore be reduced to: adhering strictly to planned fertilizer goals, increasing machinery stocks by lowering retirement rates, taking pains that planned gains from land reclamation projects -- especially in the Non-Black Soil Zone -- are realized, and possibly stimulating the private sector. Even this program does not guarantee success. Efforts to stabilize output through land reclamation projects will increase the cost of production but will only marginally contribute to stability. And the continual drop in rural population means that stimulation of the private sector will in the future yield less spectacular results than it has in the past.

Agriculture clearly needs a breakthrough, primarily in agrotechnology. In view of the prospective slower growth in supplies of material inputs and skilled labor as well as less favorable weather, the answer would seem to lie in better breeds, crop varieties, cultivation practices, and the like. But here also current programs appear misdirected. A September 1976 resolution on agro-science policy criticized the Soviet agricultural research effort for unnecessary duplication of research, for wasting resources, and for being out of touch with farm problems.(41) It was especially critical of the duplication found in research programs for developing new varieties of crops and new breeds of livestock. There is no

----

(41)
    Pravda, 10 September 1976.

131

evidence that the research environment will change dramatically. Most Soviet agricultural scientists probably will continue to spend their time and resources in an attempt to duplicate research already done in other countries a decade ago. The need to direct efforts at translating new research concepts and techniques into practice continues to be ignored. Moreover, the impact of advanced agricultural technology purchased from Western countries will likely be eroded by the USSR's inherent problems in assimilating foreign technology on a large scale. The lack of promise in current agricultural research programs would seem to deny the Soviets the major breakthrough needed in grain production and feeding efficiency.

What, then, does the future hold for Soviet agriculture? In the past the agricultural sector has always managed to muddle through, and muddling through may be the best that Soviet leaders can hope for between now and the mid-1980s. Certainly agricultural production will be sufficient to cover much, and in some years all, of the country's food requirements. But domestic output is unlikely to be sufficient to support the progress in per capita consumption of quality foods, particularly meat, planned by the leadership and expected by consumers. As Soviet consumers become increasingly addicted to meat, the USSR will have to rely on foreign grain to support the habit. On average, perhaps as much as 10 million to 15 million tons of grain will be needed, with 20 million to 25 million tons needed in poor harvest years. Should the leadership be forced to take account of the anticipated gap between planned meat production and effective demand for meat, imports would have to be even larger, perhaps ranging up to 35 million tons. Sporadic purchases of meat may also be necessary to augment domestic production after more severe harvest shortfalls. The current regime seems willing to make at least a limited commitment, and, as long as it does, consumers will make progress. Into the 1980's, however, the relatively bleak prospects for the rest of the economy and the possibility of substantial oil imports will put the squeeze on hard currency supplies. If such a situation materializes, the leadership will have little choice. Consumers will have to be satisfied with available supplies, measuring their lot against earlier years rather than international consumption levels, particularly as the rate of improvement in other areas of consumption will also slow as the economy slows.

5

THE MILITARY BURDEN AND ARMS CONTROL

Daniel Gallik

U.S. Arms Control and Disarmament Society

The questions surrounding the economic dimensions of the Soviet military effort, the trends in such measures, and their economic and political significance, are among the most difficult that can be addressed to the Soviet economy. It is no accident that this has long been the case; it is due primarily to the exceptional secretiveness with which these matters are treated in the Soviet Union. There has been virtually no change in the stringently enforced non-disclosure policy for the military area concomitant with the changes in the Soviet Union's politico-military status in the world. In fact, as Soviet power has expanded absolutely and relatively, the contrast with the scant information made available has become more disconcerting and made questions of its economic dimensions all the more acute.

The present chapter will not attempt to provide specific answers and certainly not definitive ones. The purpose of this brief examination is as much to give the reader some idea of what we don't know as of what we do. It will touch on the state of the art in Soviet military expenditure estimation, proceed to relative measures of military effort or its economic shares of the economy, to the burden or drag that it has on the economy both objectively and subjectively perceived, and finally examine some of the reciprocal implications among military effort levels, economic concerns, and arms control.

----

(1)
The views and judgements expressed are the author's alone and do not necessarily reflect those of that Agency or any other department or agency of the U.S. Government. The invaluable support, suggestions, and editing of Holland Hunter are gratefully acknowledged.

133

MILITARY EXPENDITURES

As most readers should be aware, the extremely limited information published by the Soviet Union explicitly on military-economic matters consists almost literally of one word and one number in the annual budget -- that is, the allocation for "defense" = X number of rubles. Furthermore, even well-informed observers inside or outside the U.S.S.R. cannot interpret this information with any confidence. As a result, obtaining basic military expenditure data is a complex, difficult, uncertain, and often controversial matter of estimation.

Among Western observers in the early 1970's, the official Soviet figure of about 17 to 18 billion rubles for annual defense outlays was usually adjusted upward to include such items as R&D on defense and space (placed in the science category of the budget) for a total of around 24 billion rubles. Other observers compiling a total by other means reached about twice this level.(2) In 1976, CIA repriced its estimates of Soviet defense outlays in ruble terms and arrived at a 1970 level in the range of 40 to 50 billion rubles. Their upward adjustment reflected almost entirely the assignment of higher costs and ruble prices to the same real flows of defense-related output, with something like 10% of the rise reflecting a higher assessment of product quality. The dollar equivalent of this aggregate ruble estimate remained essentially unchanged. Some US headlines greatly exaggerated and misinterpreted the change, giving the impression that in real terms the USSR had suddenly doubled its defense effort.

Though most Western estimates for 1970 now fall within this range of 40 to 50 billion rubles, trends before and since that date remain a matter of considerable disagreement. The CIA has not yet released revised estimates for prior years, but they place the growth rate in subsequent years at four to five percent annually, with a 1975 level of some 55 to 60

----

(2)

For a good sample of the literature, see the papers by Robert W. Campbell et al., Stanley H. Cohn, Earl R. Brubaker, and Herbert Block in U.S. Congress, Joint Economic Committee, <u>Soviet Economic Prospects for the Seventies</u>, June 27, 1973, pp. 122-204.

billion rubles in constant 1970 prices.(3) On the other hand, another long time analyst of these problems, William T. Lee, places the 1970-75 growth rate at about ten percent and the 1966-70 rate at about twelve percent.(4) Thus, in spite of a slight slowdown in growth rate, he reaches a range of 71 to 81 billion constant 1970 rubles for his 1975 expenditure estimate.

The differences reflect alternative estimating methodologies, each of which has its merits. This is not the time or place for extended discussion of these methodologies, but it seems clear that whatever agreement may have existed concerning the 1970 level of Soviet defense spending, it has already given way to considerable divergence among outside observers. This means, unfortunately, that all aspects of available Soviet military expenditure estimates -- coverage, level, growth rates, component details, conversion to or from real or dollar terms -- should be viewed with much skepticism and with allowance for wide margins of error. This is not to suggest that nothing can be done about it; these margins could and should be substantially reduced. Progress would require large, vigorous, and imaginative research efforts, but they would be well worth making in view of their importance for domestic and international policy.

ECONOMIC IMPACT

The most common measure of economic impact, the ratio of military spending to GNP, is estimated by the CIA to have been 11% to 13%(5) and by Lee to have been about 12% around 1970. The CIA's ratio for subsequent years remains constant while Lee's rises to 14% to 15% by 1975. These are all very substantial shares. They compare, for example, with a world median ratio in 1975 of 2.5%, a third quartile level of 5%,

----

(3)
    C.I.A., Estimated Soviet Defense Spending in Rubles, 1970-1975, SR 76-101210, May 1976.
(4)
    William T. Lee, The Estimation of Soviet Defense Expenditures, 1955-1975: An Unconventional Approach, Praeger, 1977.
(5)
    Joint Economic Committee, Congress of the United States, Allocation of Resources in the Soviet Union and China - 1977, Part 3, June 23 and 30 (Executive Sessions), and July 6, 1977. Testimony of the C.I.A. Director, Adm. Stansfield Turner.

and an international high of 38% in Israel. The ratio for the
United States in 1975 was about 5%, while in 1967, near the
peak of Vietnam outlays, it was 9.5%(6)

Another useful relative measure of impact is the ratio of
military employment to total employment. The CIA has made
estimates in the past using input-output tables which make it
possible to estimate the civilian labor input that goes
directly into the production of defense goods, as well as all
the indirect labor needed in every corner of the economy to
support the direct defense production activity. Adding this
labor to the number in armed forces and the estimated number
of civilians employed by the Ministry of Defense produces a
grand total of all military-related labor in the economy. For
1970, this approach indicated that some 9% of the labor force
was directly or indirectly involved in defense-related
employment. Given the C.I.A.'s revised estimates of ruble
expenditures for procurement and other nonpersonnel
expenditures, this ratio may now be more like 12%. By way of
comparison, a similar share of defense-supporting employment
in the United States reached almost 10% in 1968, at the peak
of Vietnam involvement; presently it is about 6%.(7) Using
similar input-output techniques, the C.I.A. has estimated that
around 1975 military requirements, both direct and indirect,
accounted for the following shares of output in major branches
of Soviet heavy industry.(8)

Energy 1/6

Chemicals 1/6

Metallurgy 1/5

Machinery and metal working . . . 1/3

----

(6)

U.S. Arms Control and Disarmament Agency, World Military
Expenditures and Arms Transfers, 1966-1975, G.P.O., 1977.

(7)

Richard Oliver, "Employment Effects of Reduced Defense
Spending," Monthly Labor Review, December, 1971; and
Department of Labor, Bureau of Labor Statistics, Foreign
Defense Sales and Grants, Fiscal Years 1973-1975: Labor
and Material Requirements, July 1977.

(8)

C.I.A., Estimated Soviet Defense Spending in Rubles,
1970-1975, SR 76-101210, May 1976.

These too are very large shares. In specialized branches of industry such as electronics and instruments, where integrated circuitry, computers, and other advanced technology are involved, the military share of output is well over one-half.

Especially striking is the machinery figure, in view of that industry's importance for capital goods production and hence for economic growth. The estimate that 33% of machinery output goes to defense still does not conceptually measure the full impact. It covers the direct military purchases from the machinery industry of military investment goods, such as arms and supporting equipment, and of items like spare parts needed for operations. It also covers the machinery industry output purchased by all other industries for use in supplying the military with their goods -- that is, their direct and indirect requirements for machinery on current account, as can be calculated only with the help of input-output tables. However, this estimate omits another substantial military drain on machinery output. The arms-producing portion of the machinery industry can be conceived of as a separate sector capable of serving only the military, at least in the short and medium term. Therefore, machinery output consisting of new and replacement capital for this arms-producing sector should be charged as an additional defense-induced drain on the machinery industry.

ECONOMIC BURDEN

What has been the burden, the retarding effect, of the military program on the Soviet economy? It is frequently argued that the U.S.S.R. has a two-track economy, one military and one civilian, and that the two are insulated from each other. The military economy is seen as providing little stimulus or guidance for the civilian economy; spillovers are thought to be inhibited by a wall of secrecy separating defense-related production from the surrounding economy.(9)

Until recently, the military part of the economy was thought to be much more efficient, because it had higher priorities for high quality inputs of labor and materials, more effective organization, stricter quality controls, etc. The civilian part of the economy by contrast was seen as

----

(9)
    See Robert W. Campbell, "Management Spillovers from Soviet Space and Military Programmes," Soviet Studies, April 1972, pp. 590-602.

having a residual claim to lower-grade materials and labor managed inefficiently at higher real costs. This view of a more efficient military sector has now lost much of its currency, partly because current evidence on the costs and prices of defense-related end products does not indicate much of an efficiency differential in their favor. The issue is conceptually intricate; a high ruble price could reflect inefficient production generating high costs, or it could measure superior quality and effectiveness of the product.

To the extent that military support sectors enjoy various intangible advantages over civilian sectors that are not reflected in the quantities of resources they are allocated, in recognized costs, or in the prices they receive, any relative efficiency of these military sectors is partly illusory. Nevertheless, some analysts hold that the opportunity costs of these advantages are low because they could not be effectively transferred to the civilian economy even if budget and resources allocations should be so transferred.

This argument seems overdrawn and deserves further research. For example, Gur Ofer found that such nonmonetary advantages in the military R&D sector were more important than generally credited and that most of them result from conscious policy decisions rather than "natural" or inherent factors.(10) In his view, the organization of the Soviet economy is especially suited to carry out the transfers of such advantages to the civilian sector effectively.

It seems incontestable that, however uncertain the precise dimensions, the Soviet military sector has had a serious negative impact on the surrounding economy, and that this has been true for half a century. It is not only that resources devoted to defense could have been devoted instead to consumer welfare in the short run. More importantly, long-run expansion of Soviet productive capacity has been distorted and held back by diversion of resources into military end-uses. Four or five decades ago, the distortion seemed justified by the threat of war, and in retrospect we know that Soviet survival in World War II was not unrelated to her pre-war defense effort. It remains true, nonetheless, that when an insulated military sector deprives the surrounding economy of high quality inputs in large volume,

----

(10)
    Gur Ofer, The Opportunity Cost of the Nonmonetary Advantages of the Soviet Military R&D Effort, RAND Report R-1741-DDRE, August 1975.

138

especially of new technology, healthy economic growth is hobbled and improved living standards are undermined.(11.)

PERCEIVED BURDEN

Even if the impact of the military sector in the objective sense significantly dampens and distorts the economy's expansion, the influence on Soviet national policy will depend, for one thing, on the extent of awareness of this burden, and, for another, on official perceptions of the offsetting benefits that flow from Soviet military efforts.

Awareness of the objective burden, at least in the more knowledgeable circles, may be greater than is usually thought in the West. Indications of such awareness are heavily censored, of course, but they show through in scattered fashion among emigres, in the more candid personal contacts, and in print. The very pervasiveness of military programs must be telling; 60 percent of Soviet enterprises are said to be engaged in military production.(12) There are circumstantial factors accounting for a greater awareness since the late-50s and early-60s. One can cite economic factors, such as the 1967 price reforms, which may have served in part to expose more accurately than before the true costs of defense-related products. Interest in economic modeling and more rational economic planning inevitably leads to more explicit concerns -- by a broader range of planners, analysts, and decisionmakers -- with the defense impact on the surrounding economy. There is also the influence of political discussions about military "parity" and detente, as well as publicity on military and space achievements, with the military connotation of the latter in the Soviet context. Nevertheless, there is little evidence of a conscious or articulated awareness of the burden among the general public.

The trend of Soviet perceptions of the burden at the official level is far harder to evaluate. If the share of Soviet GNP devoted to defense has remained constant, it seems obvious after the fact that Soviet authorities have not been forced to reduce it. The continued high rate of spending in

----

(11)
Compare the discussion in Joint Economic Committee, Congress of the United States, Soviet Economic Problems and Prospects, August 1977, pp. 9, 16, and 19-21.
(12)
Boris Rabbot, "Detente: The Struggle Within," Washington Post, July 10, 1977, pp. B1-B5.

the 60s and 70s indicates that the burden laid on the people
and on the economy's growth potential has seemed worthwhile,
at least so far, to the top decisionmakers. The absolute
volume of real resources made available to the military sector
has expanded to a formidable extent. If this growth, properly
measured, has in fact involved a rising percentage claim on
Soviet GNP, the even stronger implication is that Soviet
decisionmakers have seen net benefits in tightening up on
other claims.

SOME IMPLICATIONS AND INTERACTIONS

Assuming the objective existence of a heavy military
burden in the USSR, and a sufficient awareness of the burden
in official quarters, its evaluation will depend heavily on
the course of the economic difficulties under review in this
book and recognized elsewhere.(13) The greater the
difficulties, the more onerous will be the perceived impact of
any given level and trend of military effort. A bouyant and
expansive economy can obviously bear a heavier burden than a
faltering and strained economy.

Present conditions and prospects therefore confer a new
degree of significance on the kinds of arms control options
that now deserve consideration. If a Soviet intention to
drive for immediate military superiority is assumed, then arms
control will have little relevance to Soviet perceptions. But
if basic economic power plays a large role in Soviet strategy,
as it historically appears to have done, then contributors to
economic vigor -- healthy growth rates, a capacity to generate
and assimilate innovations, a reduction of the Soviet lag
behind the West, etc. -- also play a much larger role.

In this context, the kinds of arms control options that
shape the environment of current discussions become important
influences on perceptions of burden. For example, available
prospects for broader or overall limits going beyond specific
individual weapons systems, and bearing on current Soviet
concern with the technological gap and impending economic
retardation, should make the arms burden seem heavier.

----

(13)
Joint Economic Committee, Congress of the United States,
Soviet Economic Problems and Prospects, August 1977; and
Abram Bergson, "The Soviet Economic Slowdown," Challenge,
January - February, 1978.

Are there such broad types of limits available? Not in any practical sense at present. Overall military expenditure limitations, to take one obvious example, seem to founder immediately on the conflict between their requirements for large amounts of detailed data, necessary for purposes of comparative measurement and verification, and the traditional Soviet policy of non-disclosure.(14) A number of other arms control concepts encounter the same obstacle. The Western countries have therefore shown little interest in such measures (beyond a willingness to explore their feasibility and to promote favorable conditions), as long as Eastern non-disclosure appears so firmly entrenched. The East, on the other hand, may see little to gain by changing, in view of the apparent relative lack of Western interest in broad limitations. However, if this chicken-and-egg dilemma should somehow be surmounted, broad types of limitations in the mutual interests of both sides may be possible.(15)

----

(14)
    Abraham S. Becker, <u>Military Expenditure Limitation for Arms Control: Problems and Prospects</u>, Ballinger, 1977.
(15)
    See Barry Blechman et al., <u>The Soviet Military Buildup and U.S. Defense Spending</u>, The Brookings Institution, Washington, D.C., 1977, particularly pp. 7-14, 21-25, and 54-61 for a discussion of the interaction of the Soviet buildup and U.S. efforts.

6
LABOR SUPPLY CONSTRAINTS AND RESPONSES

Philip Grossman
Central Intelligence Agency

<u>INTRODUCTION</u>

The specter of labor shortages throughout the 1980s must be especially painful to Soviet planners because of their past heavy dependence on labor for economic growth. Indeed, labor force growth since World War II has been considerably faster in the USSR than in the United States and Western Europe, while productivity growth has been considerably slower. In this connection, a Western observer of the Soviet economic scene has commented that the ultimate test of the Soviet system will be its ability to elicit favorable productivity responses to offset unfavorable manpower trends, and thereby sustain its economic growth.(1)

In this chapter, Soviet population trends and prospects are summarized, the nature and magnitude of the unfavorable manpower trends are described, and the policy options available to the Soviet leadership are evaluated, with special attention to their implication for economic growth.

<u>POPULATION TRENDS AND VITAL RATES</u>

The Soviet population, estimated at 261.4 million in mid-1978, has been increasing at an average annual rate of less than one percent since the mid-1960s (Table 6.1). Population growth peaked at 1.8% annually during the late 1950s, when the death rate was still falling and the birth rate was holding fairly steady. Subsequently, the birth rate

----

(1)

Stanley H. Cohn, "The Soviet Path to Economic Growth: A Comparative Analysis," <u>Review of Income and Wealth</u>, Series 22, No. 1, March 1976, pp. 49-59.

TABLE 6.1
USSR: Estimates and Projections of the Population
and Vital Rates

	Population (Mid-Year, in Millions)	Population Growth Rate (Percent)	Birth Rate (Percent)	Death Rate (Percent)
1950	180.1	1.70	2.67	0.97
1960	214.3	1.83	2.49	0.71
1970	242.8	0.92	1.74	0.82
1971	245.1	0.99	1.78	0.82
1972	247.5	0.94	1.78	0.85
1973	249.7	0.90	1.76	0.87
1974	252.1	0.95	1.80	0.87
1975	254.4	0.89	1.81	0.93
1976	256.7	0.90	1.84	0.94
1977	259.0	0.91	1.86	0.95
1978	261.4	0.92	1.88	0.96
1979	263.8	0.93	1.90	0.97
1980	266.3	0.94	1.92	0.98
1981	268.8	0.95	1.93	0.98
1982	271.4	0.94	1.93	0.99
1983	273.9	0.93	1.93	1.00
1984	276.5	0.91	1.91	1.00
1985	279.0	0.88	1.89	1.01
1986	281.4	0.85	1.86	1.01
1987	283.7	0.81	1.82	1.02
1988	286.0	0.77	1.79	1.02
1989	288.1	0.74	1.76	1.02
1990	290.2	0.71	1.73	1.02

Source: Unpublished data of Foreign Demographic Analysis
Division, U.S. Department of Commerce. Projections for 1976-90
assume a constant gross reproduction rate and declining
mortality weighted by age and sex.

fell by almost one-third between 1960 and 1970 and had increased only slightly by 1978, while the death rate has risen steadily and was approaching the level recorded in 1950.

Despite a declining population growth rate, the USSR still ranks with the fastest growers among Communist countries, and has a more rapidly growing population than most major developed countries. (Table 6.2) Its fertility is relatively low for a Communist country, but high for a developed one. Life expectancy for females is roughly the same as in both sets of countries, while for males it is significantly lower -- the latter a reflection of unusually high death rates among men 25-54 compared with other developed countries (Table 6.3). Furthermore, these rates have been increasing in the USSR in recent years. Soviet demographers no doubt are investigating these developments, but thus far have not publicized their findings.

Population growth has been slower in the Russian Republic (RSFSR) than in the other 14 republics, but the RSFSR still represents more than half the total population (Tables 6.4 and 6.5). The central Asian republics, and Armenia, Azerbaydzhan, and Kazakhstan are by far the fastest growing republics. Population growth in Central Asia (3%) actually is similar to growth in predominantly Moslem nations of the Near East and South Asia. Birth rates are higher, and death rates generally lower, in the cited republics, reflecting the predominantly rural environment as well as cultural traditions.

Assuming constant fertility and declining mortality, the Soviet population will increase at an average annual rate of 0.9% during the 1980s, about the same as the 1970s. However, the rate will decline steadily after 1981 as the crude birth rate declines and the crude death rate increases (Table 6.1). The decline in the birth rate is explained by the changing age structure of the population. While fertility is assumed to remain unchanged, the number of females in the prime childbearing ages declines as a share of the total population. Similarly, while mortality is assumed to decline, the age structure shifts in favor of older age groups with higher death rates. Consequently, annual population growth will decline to 0.7% in 1990 compared with 0.9% in 1980.

Under similar assumptions about population growth by republic, the disparity between growth rates in the RSFSR and most other republics will widen during the 1980s. Population growth will actually accelerate in Central Asia and the Transcaucasus, in contrast with the trend in most other republics (Table 6.5). By 1990, moreover, the population of the RSFSR will be less than half the total population.

TABLE 6.2
Population Growth, Fertility, and Life Expectancy,
Selected Countries

Country	Population Growth (a) (Percent)	Fertility(b)	Life Expectancy at Birth (Years) Male	Female
United States	0.8	60.4	68.2	75.9
Canada	1.4	61.0	69.3	76.4
Japan	1.2	67.0	71.2	76.3
Austria	0.3	57.3	67.4	74.7
Belgium	0.3	56.9	67.8	74.2
France	0.8	72.0	68.6	76.4
FRG	0.4	43.9	67.6	74.1
United Kingdom	0.2	55.7	67.8	73.8
Yugoslavia	0.9	67.9	65.4	70.2
Bulgaria	0.3	67.9	68.6	73.9
Czechoslovakia	0.6	75.8	66.5	73.5
GDR	-0.2	45.4	68.9	74.2
Hungary	0.4	69.6	66.9	72.6
Poland	0.9	69.3	66.8	73.8
Romania	0.9	79.4	66.8	71.3
USSR	0.9	67.8	64.0	74.0

a. Average annual rate of growth, 1971-75.
b. Number of live births per thousand women 15-49.

Sources: United Nations, Demographic Yearbook 1975 and (for the USSR) official Soviet sources. Data are most recent reported to the UN, and relate generally to the period 1971-75.

TABLE 6.3
Death Rates Among Males and Females, Ages 25-54,
Selected Countries (Deaths Per Thousand Persons)

Age Group	USSR 1973-74	US 1974	Japan 1974	FRG 1973	Czechoslovakia 1973	GDR 1974
			Males			
25-29	3.1	2.0	1.1	1.4	1.6	1.3
30-34	4.4	2.1	1.4	1.7	1.9	1.6
35-39	5.4	2.9	2.1	2.4	2.7	2.1
40-44	7.4	4.3	3.3	3.8	4.5	3.3
45-49	9.7	7.1	4.6	5.7	6.8	5.0
50-54	13.9	10.7	6.7	9.0	11.1	8.9
			Females			
25-29	0.9	0.8	0.7	0.7	0.6	0.6
30-34	1.4	1.0	0.8	0.9	0.8	0.9
35-39	1.8	1.6	1.2	1.3	1.2	1.2
40-44	2.6	2.5	1.7	2.1	2.0	1.9
45-49	3.7	3.8	2.6	3.3	3.3	3.3
50-54	5.8	5.6	4.0	5.0	5.2	5.0

Source: United Nations, Demographic Yearbook 1975 and, for the USSR, Vestnik Statistiki, No. 11, 1975.

TABLE 6.4
USSR: Population, by Republic (Mid-Year in Millions)

	1970	1975	1980	1985	1990
USSR, Total	242.8	254.4	266.4	279.5	291.5
RSFSR	130.4	134.2	138.4	142.1	144.0
Ukraine	47.3	48.9	50.2	51.1	51.9
Belorussia	9.0	9.4	9.7	10.1	10.4
Moldavia	3.6	3.8	4.1	4.3	4.5
Baltic republics	6.9	7.2	7.4	7.5	7.6
Estonia	1.5	1.5	1.5	1.5	1.5
Latvia	2.5	2.5	2.5	2.5	2.5
Lithuania	3.1	3.3	3.4	3.5	3.6
Central Asian republics	20.1	23.1	26.8	31.3	36.8
Kirghiziya	3.0	3.3	3.8	4.3	4.8
Tadzhikistan	2.9	3.4	4.0	4.7	5.6
Turkmenia	2.2	2.5	2.9	3.4	4.1
Uzbekistan	12.0	13.9	16.1	18.9	22.3
Transcaucasian republics	12.4	13.3	14.5	15.9	17.5
Armenia	2.5	2.8	3.1	3.4	3.8
Azerbaydzhan	5.2	5.6	6.2	7.0	7.9
Georgia	4.7	4.9	5.2	5.5	5.8
Kazakhstan	13.1	14.3	15.5	17.2	18.8

Source: Foreign Demographic Analysis Division, U.S.
Department of Commerce (unpublished preliminary data).
Projections beyond 1975 assume constant fertility and
declining mortality. Detailed data may not add to totals
showns because of rounding.

TABLE 6.5
USSR: Population Growth, by Republic
(Average Annual Rate in Percentages)

	1971-75	1976-80	1981-85	1986-90
USSR, Total	0.9	0.9	1.0	0.8
RSFSR	0.6	0.6	0.5	0.3
Ukraine	0.7	0.5	0.4	0.3
Belorussia	0.9	0.6	0.8	0.6
Moldavia	1.1	1.5	0.9	0.9
Baltic republics	0.9	0.5	0.3	0.3
Estonia	Negl.	Negl.	Negl.	Negl.
Latvia	Negl.	Negl.	Negl.	Negl.
Lithuania	1.3	0.6	0.6	0.6
Central Asian republics	2.8	3.0	3.2	3.3
Kirghiziya	1.9	2.9	2.5	2.2
Tadzhikistan	3.2	3.3	3.3	3.6
Turkmenia	2.6	3.0	3.2	3.8
Uzbekistan	3.0	3.0	3.3	3.4
Transcaucausian republics	1.4	1.7	1.9	1.9
Armenia	2.3	2.1	1.9	2.2
Azerbaydzhan	1.5	2.1	2.5	2.4
Georgia	0.8	1.2	1.1	1.1
Kazakhstan	1.8	1.6	2.1	1.8

Annual increments to the Soviet population of working age,(2) which averaged 2.5 million during 1971-75, will decline to 1.6 million in 1980 and will average less than 0.5 million in the mid-1980s. Two developments will contribute about equally to the slowdown: fewer persons reaching working age and more reaching retirement age (Table 6.6). The decline in the number of new entrants reflects the falling birth rates of the 1960s, and the increase in the number of retirees is the result of the rising birth rates of the post-revolutionary, pre-collectivization period of the 1920s.

Growth of the working-age population not only will be smaller but will be concentrated during the 1980s in Central Asia, Kazakhstan, and the Transcaucasian republics (Table 6.7). Birth rates in these republics remained relatively high during the 1960s, apparently less affected by (1) the social and economic forces reducing fertility elsewhere in the country and (2) the impact on births of World War II. As noted above, population growth rates in Central Asia, Kazakhstan, and the Transcaucasian republics traditionally have been higher than in the rest of the nation. During 1960-70, for example, those areas accounted for almost one-third of the increase of 13 million in the nation's working-age population, although they included less than one-fifth of that population.

In the RSFSR, the working-age population will actually decline during the 1980s, while it will remain essentially unchanged in the Ukraine and the Baltic region. These areas currently account for about four-fifths of the nation's nonfarm employment and an even larger share of industrial employment.

According to the 1970 census, more than 93% of males and almost 89% of females of prime working age (20-59/54) were in the work force (Table 6.8) and these shares may be even higher now. Persons of prime working age outside the work force are mainly full-time students, disabled, and residents of institutions. Practically the only potential sources of additional labor, therefore, are among the young (16-19) and the retired.

In its extensive use of women workers the USSR has gone well beyond other developed nations and even other Communist

----

(2)
Men 16 through 59 and women 16 through 54.

149

TABLE 6.6
USSR: Population of Working Age (Million Persons, Midyear)(a)

Year	Total	Annual Increments	Entrants (16-year-olds)	Deaths	Departures (55/60-year-olds)
1955	114.7	2.7	4.7	0.4	1.6
1956	116.9	2.2	4.3	0.4	1.7
1957	118.6	1.7	3.9	0.5	1.7
1958	119.6	1.0	3.1	0.4	1.7
1959	119.6	Negl.	2.1	0.4	1.7
1960	119.5	-0.1	1.9	0.2	1.8
1961	119.6	0.1	2.3	0.4	1.8
1962	120.2	0.6	2.8	0.4	1.8
1963	121.2	1.0	3.3	0.4	1.9
1964	122.6	1.4	3.8	0.4	2.0
1965	124.1	1.5	4.1	0.5	2.1
1966	125.7	1.6	4.2	0.4	2.2
1967	127.2	1.5	4.3	0.5	2.3
1968	128.6	1.4	4.4	0.6	2.4
1969	130.0	1.4	4.3	0.5	2.4
1970	131.7	1.7	4.5	0.6	2.2
1971	134.0	2.3	4.8	0.5	2.0
1972	136.5	2.5	4.9	0.5	1.9
1973	139.0	2.5	4.9	0.5	1.9
1974	141.7	2.7	5.0	0.4	1.9
1975	144.4	2.7	5.1	0.5	1.9
1976	147.1	2.7	5.2	0.6	1.9
1977	149.7	2.6	5.2	0.6	2.0
1978	152.0	2.3	5.0	0.6	2.1
1979	153.9	1.9	4.8	0.7	2.2
1980	155.5	1.6	4.6	0.6	2.4
1981	156.6	1.1	4.3	0.7	2.5
1982	157.3	0.7	4.2	0.8	2.7
1983	157.8	0.5	4.1	0.7	2.9
1984	158.2	0.4	4.0	0.7	2.9
1985	158.6	0.4	4.0	0.7	2.9
1986	158.9	0.3	4.0	0.7	3.0
1987	159.3	0.4	4.1	0.7	3.0
1988	159.9	0.6	4.2	0.7	2.9
1989	160.5	0.6	4.2	0.7	2.9
1990	161.1	0.6	4.3	0.7	3.0

a. Males age 16-59, females age 16-54.

Source: Foreign Demographic Analysis Division, U.S.
Department of Commerce. (Unpublished preliminary data).
Because of rounding, components may not add to totals shown.

TABLE 6.7
USSR: Increments to the Working Age Population
(Males 16-59, Females 16-54) in Eight Areas (in Millions)

	1971-75	1976-80	1981-85	1986-90
USSR, Total	12.7	11.1	3.2	2.5
RSFSR	5.9	4.5	-0.3	-0.7
Ukraine	1.7	1.2	-0.1	0.1
Belorussia	0.5	0.4	0.1	(a)
Moldavia	0.2	0.2	0.1	0.1
Baltic republics (b)	0.3	0.2	(a)	(a)
Central Asia republics (c)	2.0	2.3	2.0	2.0
Kazakhstan	1.1	1.1	0.7	0.6
Transcaucasian republics (d)	1.0	1.1	0.7	0.5

a. Less than 50,000.
b. Estonia, Latvia, and Lithuania
c. Kirghiziya, Tadzhikistan, Turkmenia, and Uzbekistan
d. Armenia, Azerbaydzhan, and Georgia.

Note: Details may not add to totals shown because of
rounding.

nations (Table 6.8). Until the 1960s, the participation rate of women 20 to 54 years in the USSR -- 77% in 1959 -- was about in line with other Communist nations. A large increase -- almost 12 percentage points -- between 1959 and 1970 was the principal reaction to the unusually high demand for labor during those years. As shown in Table 6.9, increments to employment actually exceeded increments to the population of working age in every year from 1959 to 1970.

The relatively low participation rates for both men and women in the retirement ages shown in Table 6.8 are probably illusory for the most part, because they pertain only to those pensioners employed in regular, full-time jobs. Because of the statutory limitations on combined monthly incomes from pension and wages, most working pensioners have part-time jobs and are classified as "pensioners" rather than as being in the labor force.

Various incentives already encourage retired persons to continue working, and demand for their services probably will increase as the increments to the working-age population dwindle. Because of limitations imposed on total earnings, working pensioners probably tend to be those with relatively small pensions and therefore with little education and skill.(3) Most collective-farm pensioners, for example, tend to continue working at least on a seasonal basis.

A slowdown in the growth of full-time enrollment in secondary and higher schools increased the supply of labor among teenagers during 1959-63 when the Soviets tinkered with a scheme that encouraged school-plus-work arrangements for Soviet youths. But educational quality deteriorated and the program was abandoned in 1964. Since then, educational policy has emphasized universal secondary education, and labor force participation rates among teenagers declined from 70% in 1959 to about 50% currently.

Considering the population and other constraints on employment growth in the U.S.S.R. during 1976-90, a slowdown

----

(3)
    The ceiling is 300 rubles per month. Average monthly earnings of professional and technical workers in industry are now more than 200 rubles monthly with experienced older workers earning much more. Pensions range from 50% to 75% of preretirement earnings, with a maximum pension of 120 rubles. These highly skilled personnel in the retirement ages, therefore, probably would gross 400 to 500 rubles or more monthly without the earnings ceiling.

152

TABLE 6.8
Economically Active Population as Percent of Total Population,
Selected Countries

	Males, 20-59	Females, 20-54	Males, 60+	Females, 55+
United States (1970)	90.9	50.4	40.4	24.7
Japan (1970)	95.2	58.3	65.5	34.7
Austria (1971)	93.8	54.8	19.8	12.1
Belgium (1970)	91.6	40.2	25.0	7.1
France (1968)	92.3	47.7	34.5	20.3
West Germany (1970)	94.4	49.8	34.0	15.4
United Kingdom (1970)	96.3	54.8	42.7	20.7
Bulgaria (1965)	92.7	81.6	35.1	18.4
Czechoslovakia (1970)	94.9	78.3	21.6	15.7
East Germany (1971)	96.0	78.3	44.2	24.3
Hungary (1970)	94.6	66.4	26.2	14.5
Poland (1970)	93.7	77.2	66.7	46.2
Romania (1966)	95.7	76.7	50.4	37.0
Yugoslavia (1971)	90.5	49.1	55.3	20.5
USSR (1970)	93.2	88.9	20.0	12.6

Source: International Labour Office, Year Book of Labour Statistics, 1975.

153

TABLE 6.9
USSR: Annual Increments to the Working Age Population
and Changes in Employment (in Millions)

Year	Working Age Population	Employment		
		Total	Agriculture	Non-Agriculture
1956	2.2	2.7	1.0	1.7
1957	1.7	1.1	-0.8	1.9
1958	1.0	2.2	0.1	2.1
1959	---	0.3	-2.0	2.3
1960	-0.1	1.4	-1.5	2.9
1961	0.1	2.6	-0.5	3.1
1962	0.6	1.8	-0.3	2.1
1963	1.0	1.2	-0.9	2.1
1964	1.4	2.6	---	2.5
1965	1.5	4.5	1.4	3.1
1966	1.6	2.7	0.1	2.6
1967	1.5	2.0	-0.6	2.6
1968	1.4	2.1	-0.6	2.7
1969	1.4	1.7	-0.9	2.6
1970	1.7	2.0	-0.2	2.2
1971	2.3	2.0	-0.3	2.3
1972	2.5	1.9	-0.4	2.3
1973	2.5	2.1	0.1	2.0
1974	2.7	2.1	---	2.1
1975	2.7	na	na	2.1

Sources: Table 6, above, and Stephen Rapawy, Estimates and
Projections of the Labor Force and Civilian Employment in the
U.S.S.R., 1950 to 1990, Foreign Economic Report No. 10, U.S.
Department of Commerce, Sept. 1976.

seems inevitable. Labor force projections prepared by Stephen Rapawy and based on constant 1970 participation rates(4) show a steady growth retardation from about 1-1/2% annually during the mid-1970s to about 1/2% toward the late 1980s -- roughly in line with growth of the working-age population.

An assumption of constant participation rates seems reasonable. As the following discussion of policy options suggests, more employment among persons in the retirement ages is likely to be offset by less employment among women 20 to 54 years of age, while the employment rate among teenagers remains unchanged. The government can be expected to legislate incentives for older workers to remain employed or return to their jobs. Rising family incomes, however, are likely to induce more Soviet women to opt for a housewife's role rather than paid employment. Furthermore, no appreciable change is envisioned in the size of the armed forces. Some modification of the conscription system is likely by 1979 or soon thereafter to accomodate shrinking cohorts of 18-years-olds, but this would yield a relatively small windfall for the civilian job market. Nor is any deliberate reduction in the school-leaving age expected; the government is not likely to reduce the educational attainment of new labor market entrants or expand work-study programs after the unfavorable experience of the early 1960s.

Barring large-scale inter-republic migration, labor force growth will exceed the national average in Central Asia, Kazakhstan, and the Transcaucasian republics, and will be negative in the Russian republic by the 1980s. Ironically, labor force participation rates exceed the national average in the Russian republic, while relatively fewer women tend toward paid employment in Central Asia.

POLICY OPTIONS AVAILABLE TO THE SOVIET LEADERSHIP

In the face of declining labor force growth and little slack in participation rates, the Soviet government is likely to launch a major effort to reduce labor demand and promote labor-saving innovations throughout the economy. Such a scenario would represent a dramatic departure from past growth strategy, which depended predominantly on rapid increases in

----

(4)
Stephen Rapawy, Estimates and Projections of the Labor Force and Civilian Employment in the U.S.S.R., 1950 to 1990, Foreign Economic Report No. 10, U.S. Department of Commerce, September 1976, pp. 14-22.

capital stock and employment. Nevertheless, the potential for labor-saving innovation in the Soviet economy is large, while the potential for maintaining employment growth at past rates is small. The government may also try to accelerate internal migration, both from rural to urban areas and from areas of relatively high labor force growth to low-growth areas.

Increasing Participation Rates

The potential for maintaining employment growth at past rates by increasing participation rates is extremely limited. The share of women 20 to 54 years of age currently in the labor force -- about 90% -- is almost as high as the share of men and probably has reached its maximum. Moreover, Moscow is not likely to tinker again with its educational system -- as it did in the early 1960s -- by promoting part-time schooling while flooding the labor market with part-time, unskilled workers in their middle teens. With regard to retirees, a dramatic change in retirement laws -- such as postponing retirement or removing the income limitation -- is essential if the retirement-age population is to be used to augment labor force growth substantially. Any change would have to be aimed specifically at urban workers who generally have little incentive to continue working under current regulations.

Partially Demobilizing the Armed Forces

A partial demobilization would augment civilian employment but would require changes in both Soviet perceptions of defense requirements and in the current policy of universal military service. Furthermore, any reduction would have to be substantial to have a significant impact on a civilian work force that currently numbers about 130 million persons on an average annual basis.(5)

Timing would be crucial in any event. When the USSR reduced its armed forces from almost 6 million in 1955 to 4 million in 1960, the windfall gain for civilian enterprises was negated in part by rising unemployment among teenagers. The planners apparently had not considered the impact of the reductions on the labor supply, and managers tended to choose seasoned veterans over inexperienced youths. The unemployed

----

(5)
    Ibid., p. 40.

were absorbed only when population growth slowed while labor demand remained high.(6)

The armed forces could be reduced gradually by reducing the number of draftees while holding the discharge rate unchanged. This would require a reversal of the policy of universal military training explicit in the 1967 military draft law. At that time, when the number of persons reaching draft age (18) was increasing rapidly, the USSR reduced mandatory service from 3 to 2 years on the average.(7) As a consequence, the number of youths drafted annually increased by about 50%. In the next 10-15 years, the opposite will happen. The numbers reaching age 18 will decline from 2.6 million in 1978 to 2.0 million in 1986-88.(8) Maintaining the size of the armed forces in the mid-1980s, therefore, will require some reduction in draft standards such as tightening deferment policies or recalling older men. To avoid such measures (and maintain the principle of universal military service) the USSR could revert to the pre-1967 terms of service. Alternatively, the decline in available draftees would provide an appropriate opportunity to cut back on the draft and thereby reduce the armed forces.

Increasing Hours of Work

Confronted by a dearth of new entrants to its work force -- especially in the 1980s -- the USSR could choose to increase its labor supply by extending the workweek from its current 41 hours. This would be a desperate measure. Stalin's extension of the workweek from 41 to 48 hours in 1940 stands as the only historical precedent in modern times. At that time, most workers had been on a 7-hour day and 41-hour week, with a "six-day" week that meant five days on and one day off, the latter changing from week to week. The 48-hour week, in force from 1940 to 1956, generally involved six 8-hour days weekly.

The reduction of weekly hours from 48 to 41 was accomplished with great fanfare during 1956-60. When it was

----

(6)
David W. Carey, "Developments in Soviet Education," Soviet Economic Prospects for the Seventies, U.S. Congress, Joint Economic Committee, 1973, p. 606.
(7)
Pravda, 25 October 1967, p. 1.
(8)
Unpublished estimates, Foreign Demographic Analysis Division, U.S. Department of Commerce.

completed, work schedules generally involved five 7-hour weekdays and a 6-hour Saturday. Then in 1967, the 41-hour workweek was compressed into five weekdays, each containing 8 hours and 12 minutes, a system that remains in effect to this day.(9)

Short of formally extending the workweek, scheduled overtime could be introduced selectively, say in priority sectors, especially by taking advantage of the availability of Saturday as a day off. But this would be an expensive procedure; labor laws dating back to the early 1930s require time-and-a-half for the first two hours of overtime, double-time thereafter and for work on holidays and days off. Furthermore, Soviet workers have grown accustomed to the current pattern of work and leisure, and would be unlikely to acquiesce placidly in any drastic change.

Inter-Republic Migration

With the population of working age increasing more rapidly in the less developed areas of Central Asia and Kazakhstan than in other areas, Soviet planners are confronted by the need for accelerated inter-republic migration. Market forces alone should stimulate some additional movement as potential workers shift to where the jobs are more plentiful and lucrative. In addition, the government still maintains an organization to handle organized recruitment and resettlement and to administer a network of labor exchanges throughout the country. The resettlement effort, however, would have to be formidable to be effective. A shift of about 9 million persons in the working ages -- presumably accompanied by their dependents -- out of Central Asia, the Transcaucasus, and Kazakhstan would be necessary during 1976-90 to make the growth of its working-age population equal to the growth in the rest of the country.(10)

Migration from these less-developed republics will have to be encouraged, and properly accomodated, if only to avoid a politically undesirable buildup of minority nationalities with relatively low income. But the orientation of these nationalities toward irrigation agriculture, warm climates and

----

(9)
David W. Bronson, "Soviet Experience with Shortening the Workweek", Industrial and Labor Relations Review, Vol. 21, No. 3, April 1968, pp. 391-99.
(10)
Based on unpublished data from the Foreign Demographic Analysis Division, U.S. Department of Commerce.

158

large families makes it unlikely that they could readily adapt to the living conditions and vocational demands of the European or Siberian regions of the country. The additional language and educational constraints make it all the more unlikely that massive westward and northward migration can be successfully achieved -- either forcibly or voluntarily.

Because of the more rapid population growth, employment growth has been faster in Central Asia, Kazakhstan, and the Transcaucasian republics than in the other republics (Tables 6.10 and 6.11). Those three regions account for about 15% of nationwide employment but contain about 20% of the total population. This discrepancy reflects lower labor force participation rates in these regions as well as a larger share of the population outside the working ages.

Rural-to-Urban Migration

Population movements from farms to cities are likely to speed up nationwide by the 1980s in response to labor shortfalls in industrial areas. Despite deliberate government efforts to slow migration by reducing rural-urban income differentials, farm incomes still are relatively low.(11) As a result, farm workers traditionally have responded to the excess labor demand in urban areas, and farm employment has declined steadily.

The movement of labor from farms to cities has often played a crucial role in sustaining relatively high manpower growth in nonagricultural sectors. Agricultural employment dropped from 43.5 million in 1958 to 38.2 million in 1964, for example, as employment opportunities swelled in urban areas because of the slow growth of the working-age population. Farm employment continued to decline, although much more slowly, into the mid-1970s.(12)

Migration from farms involved the young primarily and left behind a population predominantly outside of the working ages. Between 1959 and 1970, the rural population in the ages 20-34 declined by 33%, while the urban population in those ages increased 11% (Table 6.12). Almost half the rural

----

(11)
Gertrude E. Schroeder and Barbara S. Severin, "Soviet Consumption and Income Policies in Perspective", <u>Soviet Economy in a New Perspective</u>, U.S. Congress, Joint Economic Committee, 1976, pp. 620-660.
(12)
Rapawy, op. cit., p. 40.

TABLE 6.10
USSR: Average Annual Employment by Economic Sector in Selected Regions (In Thousands)

	USSR			Central Asia, Kazakhstan, and Transcaucasian Republics			Other Republics		
	1965	1970	1975	1965	1970	1975	1965	1970	1975
Total (a)	95,562	106,901	117,333	13,393	15,580	18,021	82,169	91,321	99,312
Industry	27,056	31,593	34,054	2,395	3,023	3,411	24,661	28,570	30,643
Agriculture (a)	27,811	25,895	25,438	4,904	4,872	5,375	22,907	21,023	20,063
Transport and Communications	8,259	9,315	10,743	1,141	1,374	1,643	7,118	7,941	9,100
Construction	5,617	9,052	10,574	970	1,485	1,684	4,647	7,567	8,890
Trade	6,009	7,537	8,857	854	1,082	1,320	5,155	6,455	7,537
Education, Science Services, and Health	13,501	16,343	18,951	2,089	2,684	3,272	11,412	13,659	15,679
Government Administration	1,460	1,883	2,243	233	297	373	1,227	1,586	1,870
Personal Services, Credit, and Insurance	2,686	3,440	4,324	351	468	607	2,335	2,972	3,717
Other	3,163	1,843	2,149	456	295	336	2,707	1,548	1,813

a. Excluding private subsidiary (agricultural) economy.

Source: Official Soviet Statistical Yearbooks.

TABLE 6.11
USSR: Average Annual Growth Rates of Employment
by Economic Sector in Selected Regions (in Percentages)

Economic Sector	Central Asia, Kazakhstan, and Transcaucasus		Other Republics	
	1966-70	1971-75	1966-70	1971-75
Agriculture (a)	-0.1	2.0	-1.7	-0.9
Industry	4.8	2.4	3.0	1.4
Construction	8.9	2.5	10.2	3.3
Transport and Communications	3.8	3.6	2.2	2.8
Trade	4.8	4.1	4.6	3.1
Education, health, and science services	6.1	4.0	3.7	2.8
Personal services, credit, and insurance	5.9	5.3	4.9	4.6
Government administration	5.0	4.7	5.3	3.3

a. Excluding private subsidiary (agricultural) economy.

Source: Derived from data in Table 10.

161

TABLE 6.12
USSR: Urban and Rural Population by Age
(Million Persons on 15 January)

Age	Urban		Rural	
	1959	1970	1959	1970
Total	100.0	136.0	108.8	105.7
0-14	26.6	33.9	35.0	36.4
15-59	65.6	88.0	61.9	54.9
15-19	8.1	13.7	8.4	8.3
20-34	30.7	34.1	26.9	17.9
35-59	26.8	40.2	26.6	28.7
60 and over	7.8	14.1	11.9	14.4

Source: Official results of the 1959 and 1970 population censuses.

162

population in 1970 was under 15 or over 59, compared with one-third in urban areas. Available demographic data suggest that migration may have accelerated since 1970. The total rural population, which declined from 109 million in 1959 to 105 million in 1970, fell further to 98 million by January 1977.(13)

THE LIKELIHOOD OF ACCELERATED PRODUCTIVITY GROWTH

The bureaucratic response to the impending slowdown in employment growth was not long in coming. The 10th five-year plan (1976-80) was given the title, "the plan of efficiency and quality." Targets for accelerating the improvement of labor utilization, such as reducing manual work through mechanization and increasing the capital-labor ratio, are included in the plan. In addition, the plan calls for altering the wage system so that payments are related more closely to results.(14)

Lacking direct controls over hiring and firing, the goverment will have to use its planning and incentive systems to influence labor allocation and utilization. In the USSR, workers are expected to find jobs on their own, with help from the labor exchanges, while enterprise managers are expected to recruit workers in accordance with plan goals. These plan goals, in turn, can be expected to reflect the growing scarcity of labor, and workers and management alike will be under considerable pressure to improve labor utilization.

The industrial sector of the economy has already demonstrated that slower employment growth need not necessarily result in a commensurately slower growth in output (Table 6.13). Some of the upsurge in labor productivity in 1971-75 may have come from shifts toward less labor-intensive processes. In the coal industry, for example, the share of surface mining -- characterized by higher output per manhour than underground mining -- increased sharply during 1971-75.(15) In addition, the "Shchekino Experiment," begun in

----

(13)
     USSR Central Statistical Administration, SSSR v Tsifrakh
     v 1976 godu, (The USSR in Figures in 1976, Moscow, 1977,
     p. 7.
(14)
     Pravda, 28 October 1976, pp. 2-3.
(15)
     USSR Central Statistical Administration, Narodnoye
     Khozyaystvo SSSR v 1975 godu, Moscow, 1976, p. 242.

TABLE 6.13
USSR: Output, Employment, and Productivity in Major Industries
(Average Annual Percentage Increase)

	Output (a)			Employment			Output per Worker		
	1961-65	1966-70	1971-75	1961-65	1966-70	1971-75	1961-65	1966-70	1971-75
INDUSTRY, TOTAL	6.7	6.7	5.7	3.9	2.9	1.5	2.7	3.7	4.1
Coal	2.8	2.0	2.3	0.1	-1.4	-2.7	2.7	3.5	5.1
Chemicals	11.6	8.7	8.9	9.6	4.6	2.3	1.8	2.9	6.5
Ferrous Metals	7.5	5.5	4.2	3.4	1.2	0.1	4.0	3.5	4.1
MBMW	7.8	8.3	7.4	6.6	3.9	2.8	1.1	4.2	4.5
Construction Materials	5.2	5.4	5.1	1.7	3.1	1.5	3.4	2.2	3.6
Forest Products	3.0	3.5	3.7	0.9	0.2	-0.4	2.1	3.3	4.1
Light Industry	2.4	8.0	2.6	2.2	3.1	0.3	0.2	4.8	2.3
Food	7.0	4.7	3.7	3.7	2.3	0.8	3.2	2.4	2.9

a. Rush V. Greenslade, "The Real Gross National Product of the USSR, 1950-1975," in Soviet Economy in a New Perspective, US Joint Economic Committee, 14 Oct. 76, p. 271.
b. Stephen Rapawy, Estimates and Projections of the Labor Force and Civilian Employment in the U.S.S.R., 1950 to 1990, Foreign Economic Report No. 10, U.S. Department of Commerce, September 1976, p. 47.

1967 as an effort to eliminate redundant labor, is now standard procedure in many industrial enterprises. Under the "experiment," wages saved by reducing employment are distributed among the remaining employed workers. Usually, redundant workers are transferred elsewhere in the enterprise, or else employment is reduced by attrition, to avoid actual dismissals.(16)

The incentive to eliminate redundant labor will grow stronger, especially in the 1980s, as increments to the labor force dwindle rapidly. The major contributing factors to "over-full employment" in the Soviet economy have been

- on the supply side, a government policy insuring jobs for all who want them,

- on the demand side, a tendency on the part of managers to hoard workers, and

- an aversion on the part of policy makers to the social and political consequences of technological unemployment.

In a tight labor market, hoarding of labor will become increasingly difficult and technological unemployment less of a concern.

Labor-saving innovations offer another means of keeping growth rates up in construction, transportation, and communications, as well as in industry. To assure an incentive structure that encourages labor-saving innovation, the "Shchekino Experiment" or some variation of it might be extended wherever possible throughout these sectors, encountering diminishing resistance as the labor market tightens. The government and enterprise traditions that have perpetuated over-full employment underlie most of the resistance to the "Experiment" encountered thus far. Given those traditions, an incentive system designed specifically to save labor could be most effective during periods of relative labor shortage.

The services sector of the economy, heavily labor-intensive and less responsive to labor-saving innovations, will require special attention from the planners.

----

(16)
    For recent discussion see S. Ivanov, "Shchekino Method in 10th Five-Year Plan," _Sotsialesticheskiy trud_, No. 4, April 1977, pp. 7-18.

Growth of services accelerated during the Brezhnev era, and continuing rapid employment growth is required for their further expansion. High teacher/pupil ratios in education, and doctor/patient ratios in health care, are examples of service measures where quality could deteriorate with labor shortfalls. Soviet planners apparently hope to hold employment growth in "productive" sectors to a minimum, thereby permitting most of the additional labor to be absorbed into the services sector.

Even if planning and tinkering with management incentive systems can bring redundant labor down to reasonable levels, the motivation of the labor force would remain as the principal uncertainty with respect to forecasts of labor productivity. Official complaints about the pace and quality of work are abundant. Some Soviet writers have argued that more consumer goods and better housing are as important as or even more important than additional capital stock in raising the productivity of labor. Real per capita consumption has been rising steadily in the USSR; the problem seems to be how to tie the rate of increase more directly to performance in the factory or on the farm.

In any event, the quest for productivity growth, especially through labor-saving innovation, will play a critical role in Soviet economic policy for the foreseeable future. The unusually wasteful use of labor in the USSR has been documented extensively in Western commentary. Planners apparently are hoping that a tighter labor supply will force managers to surface what the Soviets euphemistically call "hidden reserves" and thereby use their labor more efficiently.

7
SUMMARY OBSERVATIONS AND REFLECTIONS

Holland Hunter
Haverford College

The preceding chapters have provided a wide-ranging survey of the present situation of the Soviet economy and a judicious evaluation of its prospects for the next five or ten years. The current picture is one of an economy that has reached its present position by driving ahead fairly steadily, without much unemployment or inflation, raising output levels and living standards at quite a respectable rate. Yet Soviet economic performance is not satisfactory in the eyes of Soviet authorities, nor is it impressive in comparison with the economic performance of other successful countries. Moreover a number of basic problems have come into view as serious obstacles on the road to further progress. This brief concluding chapter offers some reflections on the resulting overall outlook and some tentative evaluation of a range of possible developments.(1)

The principal features of the Soviet economy's immediate future take their shape from the interaction of two strong contending forces. Soviet authorities are continuing to press their steady drive for economic growth, and in the process are contending against a set of serious limitations. The limitations are partly in the resource base and partly in the economy's institutional framework. The Soviet leadership is attempting to surmount these limitations both by extending the resource base and by seeking minor institutional reforms. In weighing midrun prospects, therefore, we should pull together the findings of the preceding chapters in both respects. What

----

(1)
    For an informed, critical, but more optimistic analysis, see Academician T. S. Khachaturov's book, The Economy of the Soviet Union Today, Moscow: Progress Publishers, 1977.

are the resource constraints on Soviet economic growth? What is unsatisfactory about the current composition of Soviet output? Why is it that, though declining effectiveness has stimulated several campaigns for economic reform since Stalin died, Soviet economic institutions have so far proved so stubbornly resistant to change?

CONSTRAINTS ON SOVIET GROWTH

It is clear from the age structure of the present Soviet population that for at least the next decade and a half the Soviet labor force will be growing very slowly. The explanation lies in a combination of reduced numbers of youths due to enter the labor force and an increased number of retirees due to leave the labor force, as explained in Philip Grossman's chapter. No easy remedies are available. This impending tightness in additional labor supplies will almost eliminate a major factor underlying past Soviet economic growth. Over the last half century, ample supplies of manpower and womenpower have been a key element in the expansion of non-agricultural activity in the Soviet economy. Now a new period is beginning, in which growth will have to come from other sources.

Another constraint on Soviet output growth reflects rising resource costs. The real costs of Soviet fuels and raw materials have been rising for some time and, as Douglas Whitehouse and Daniel Kazmer show in their chapter, further increases are in prospect. When high grade, conveniently located resource deposits become depleted, use of poorer supplies means that agglomeration and beneficiation costs increase. Where high grade mineral supplies are still ample, they are expensive to obtain. The USSR has immense supplies of petroleum, natural gas, coal, and many minerals in the north and east, but they lie hundreds of kilometers (even three or four thousand kilometers) from consumption centers. In spite of low ton-mile costs of freight transportation, long and increasing distances from deposit to point of use raise delivered costs. Moreover most of these northern and eastern resources must be extracted under permafrost conditions that raise formidable difficulties. The fabulous wealth of Siberia that has attracted Russians for centuries is now proving to be genuinely expensive in unanticipated ways. As a result of a shift to higher-cost resources, basic industrial output gains are harder to achieve now than they were fifty or twenty-five years ago.

A third constraint on Soviet economic expansion comes from reduced capital effectiveness. Massive increments of fixed capital plant and equipment have been a central feature

of Soviet growth since 1928. Over the last two decades,
however, the output gains obtained from further capital
increments have been gradually declining. Diminishing returns
are now painfully obvious. They have not been offset, as they
have in most developed economies, by bouyant technological
progress. This means, as Abram Bergson has demonstrated, that
any given rate of output growth requires a higher rate of
investment than it used to.(2) Since a higher fraction of
annual output must be drained off into capital formation, the
shares of output available for consumption and/or national
defense are squeezed. Current Soviet plans call for
improvements in capital effectiveness, but as Whitehouse and
Kazmer show, no marked reversal of the downward trend in
capital effectiveness is likely to emerge soon.

A fourth constraint on Soviet growth comes from an ailing
agricultural sector that wastes resources and holds the rest
of the economy back. Agriculture continues to require a
fourth of the labor force, as compared to five or ten percent
in most developed economies. Recently Soviet agriculture has
been receiving an absolutely larger flow of plant and
equipment than United States agriculture receives, yet Soviet
agricultural output remains inadequate, in Soviet as well as
Western eyes. The sector is sick, and the analysis provided
by Barbara Severin and David Carey shows that current programs
are unlikely to restore the patient to good health. Some of
the difficulties are climatic and locational, beyond easy
remedy by any known means. The main problems, however, appear
to center in a malfunctioning institutional structure.

Finally, Soviet output growth is constrained by limited
prospects in foreign trade. Soviet authorities in the last
decade have greatly expanded Soviet foreign trade, especially
with the Developed West, but the quantitative contribution of
this trade to Soviet output growth has been modest, and it
appears that further gains will not come easily. A sustained
flow of exports to cover the cost of Soviet imports can only
be extracted from the Soviet domestic economy at high
opportunity costs in other directions. Donald Green's chapter
examines the competing claims that arise from domestic
consumption and from the needs of Eastern Europe, especially
for petroleum.

----

(2)
    "Toward a New Growth Model," Problems of Communism,
    March-April 1973, pp. 1-9.

PROBLEMS IN THE COMPOSITION OF SOVIET OUTPUT

Because of continued Soviet stress on heavy industrial production, Soviet output is composed to an unusual extent of intermediate rather than final goods and services. Heavy industry produces a massive flow of fuels, raw materials, and fabricated components that go into industrial production itself. Much of what emerges as final products goes to increments of plant and equipment that serve in turn to enlarge the industrial base still further. The intangible services that account for a large part of high Western living standards are officially considered in the USSR to be "non-productive." Fifty years ago, when the industrialization drive began, it was expected that a five or ten year period of herioc efforts to build heavy industry would enable the Soviet economy to demonstrate its superiority over capitalism by delivering an abundant stream of consumer goods and services, produced by the enlarged industrial base. The shift from producer goods toward consumer goods has been long delayed, however, and the USSR still has, in Lloyd Reynold's phrase, an "input-input" economy. Thus one basic problem in the composition of Soviet output involves the unusually large place taken up by industry and an associated constraint on the availability of output for final consumption by households.

A second problem in the composition of Soviet output arises because so much of it is of poor quality. The never ending pressure for increased quantity has led harried producers for fifty years to cut corners, overlook defects, accept hasty work, and deliver shoddy production. It is extremely difficult for any individual producer to raise the quality of his product. His inputs are likely to arrive behind schedule, thus undermining his own scheduling, and what arrives is likely to have incorrect specifications and a variety of qualitative deficiencies. The manager of a construction project has to contend with poor quality cement, bricks, timber, and other components, to say nothing of an ill-trained labor force subject to rapid turnover. Railroads, trucking firms, and internal waterways deliver freight service under strained conditions that often leave shippers and receivers frustrated. Producers are thus forced to supply poor-quality output to their customers, who in turn pass a poor-quality product on to their customers in a long chain of unsatisfactory performance.

Costs and values are paradoxically summed up in this context. These massive, clumsy efforts, extending all the way from mines and forests on through to the retail level, generate a huge aggregate volume of real costs, summed up into a large and costly real GNP. Yet the usefulness of this output in a welfare sense is impaired by its low quality. One could imagine by contrast a similar aggregate of goods and services produced, say, with Western European or Japanese quality imbedded in it, that would be more "compact," use fewer real inputs, and have lower real costs. At the same time it would be more valuable in a welfare sense. While at present there is no satisfactory means of calibrating this kind of international comparison, the observation can serve as a reminder of an as-yet unachieved potential for Soviet progress. Even without any aggregate quantitative growth in GNP, cost-reducing gains in efficiency, together with qualitative improvements in commodities, would serve to make the real aggregate Soviet GNP larger in a welfare sense.

The composition of Soviet output flows over the last half century has led in cumulative fashion to another notable feature of the present Soviet economy: large deficiencies in the stock of residential capital, urban social overhead capital, and the facilities required to supply public and private social services. The state has made well-publicized efforts in these directions, especially in the last quarter century, but by comparison with the Developed West, the USSR still shows shocking deficiencies, especially in the supply of water mains, sewers, and paved streets. Retail trade facilities are inadequate in old cities and skimpily provided for in new cities. Urban housing is still in very short supply. The diversion of resources away from these basic components of an advanced society has, over several decades, facilitated rapid expansion of Soviet industrial and military power, but it has left accumulated shortfalls that will take many years to overcome under present priorities.

The structure of Soviet output displays still another striking feature: a relatively large national defense component. Though precise quantitative evidence is meager, it appears that more than a tenth, possibly an eighth, of the current Soviet GNP consists of national defense outlays. These cover both the services of some four million men and women in the armed forces, and the annual procurement of diverse forms of defense hardware. Other countries, notably Japan, are able to devote a much smaller share of their resources to national defense, and are thus able to enjoy both higher living standards and faster economic growth, using resources that have been deflected from the defense sector. In Daniel Gallik's chapter, the burden of defense on the Soviet economy is briefly reviewed. It is apparent that over the last quarter century Soviet authorities have been able to build a modern and formidable military establishment, while simultaneously the living standards of Soviet citizens were steadily improving and the economy's capital stock was expanding at an impressive rate. Guns were not obtained at the expense of butter, and the economy's

171

production-possibility frontier was not prevented from moving outward. Nevertheless non-defense gains would have been larger if the defense effort had been smaller. Under the more straitened circumstances of the 1980s, it seems obvious that there is potential for relieving pressure on other fronts, if the USSR finds it possible to shift resources from national defense into consumption and/or investment.

DILEMMAS OF ECONOMIC REFORM

Soviet efforts at economic reform are caught on the horns of a basic dilemma: can a large economy be adequately flexible and innovative while at the same time it is tightly managed by central political authority? Soviet institutions of Party and government control make up a duplicative, overlapping, and rigid mechanism for managing the economy. There is not much scope for sensitivity to the choices by households that would maximize their welfare or the choices by producers that would minimize their production costs. It is still a matter of deep ideological conviction among the system's directors that, if bureaucratic controls were relaxed and freer rein were given to a responsive market mechanism, resources would be misdirected and national purposes would suffer. Modest efforts to decentralize controls, encourage innovation, and improve responsiveness have been frustrated by the stubborn resistance of apparatchiki. New arrangements for autonomy and initiative at the enterprise level have been so rigidly codified and tightly supervised by the center that genuine independence has been smothered.(3) The regime is thus caught in a basic dilemma, desiring innovation and flexibility but unwilling in practice to abandon the controls that make the economy proof against improvement.

A closely related problem involves the incentives that motivate all the actors in the economy. Instead of encouraging and rewarding high quality production, the positive and negative incentives that are set before plant directors, middle management, foremen, and workers have the perverse effect of making low quality pay. Instead of stimulating cost-reducing or product-improving innovations, the system in practice rewards continuation of present methods. The drive for "more" overrides the desire for "better." The authorities have promulgated detailed

----

(3)
On all this, see Joseph S. Berliner's definitive analysis, The Innovation Decision in Soviet Industry, Cambridge, Mass., The MIT Press, 1976.

procedures specifically offering bonuses for bringing innovations into use, yet in practice the reward system as a whole continues to thwart progress.

Another dimension of this problem relates to the lack of slack in the system. Technological progress requires that innovations which embody scientific advances not only be carried through the research and development stage, and the stage of testing and evaluation, but also be fitted into existing production processes. This final stage has been the most difficult one in Soviet experience. Evidently much of the explanation lies in the over tautness that is chronic in Soviet industry. The down time necessary to install new methods or equipment endangers the fulfillment of current output targets. Fears concerning the length of time required to bring new equipment up to full capacity will cause the plant director, who typically operates with a very short-run time horizon, to resist the innovation. If output targets were less demanding, there would literally be more time and "adjustment space" for the introduction of an innovation that would thereafter raise output levels and improve product quality. The authorities, however, have so far been unwilling to permit this kind of slack.

Like the United States, the USSR has a "military-industrial complex," in the sense that several branches of heavy industry deliver substantial fractions of their output to national defense, and that these industrial branches form an interest group in combination with the relevant defense ministries as they compete for budgetary and other resources. The relation of this part of the Soviet economy to economic reform issues is itself quite complex. Defense-related industries and their customers would no doubt resist any substantial cuts in their share of current inputs and investment resources, of the kind that would be associated with enlarged shares for civilian consumption or non-defense investment. At the same time, if arms limitation arrangements convinced Soviet authorities that some resources could safely be shifted away from national defense, the resources might be used to raise the quality of Soviet products generally and strengthen the underlying economic base. Broad technological progress in Soviet civilian industry would indirectly serve the interests of the Soviet military-industrial complex by enhancing general economic efficiency, raising productivity, and improving industrial flexibility.

Another dilemma of reform concerns overcentralized agricultural management. The Party's long-standing hostility toward individualism in the countryside continues to thwart sensible efforts at making agriculture more productive. The technology of crop and livestock management requires timely,

173

adaptive, flexible decisionmaking in scheduling and coordinating the multiple activities of modern farming. The centralized management of Soviet agriculture is too undifferentiated, sluggish, and doctrinaire to meet these requirements effectively. Agriculture is no longer ignored in the USSR, but efforts to improve it through centralized domination continue to waste resources and produce meager results. Here too, as in the dilemma between bureaucratic controls and the market mechanism, the authorities face a choice: loosen the harness and unhook many of the overlapping reins currently hampering Soviet farms, even though the "soul of the petty-bourgeois peasant proprietor" may reappear, or retain politically secure controls at the expense of continued low productivity in agriculture.

The policy dilemma in Soviet foreign trade concerns the degree to which the authorities are willing to link the Soviet economy with the surrounding world economy. Economic independence has been costly for the USSR, not only in terms of foregone static comparative advantage, but also in terms of isolation from the ongoing industrial revolution that has made the West so hard to catch up with. In many specific industries the USSR could use imported Western processes and products to spearhead the domestic drive for technological reform and advance. Improvements in product quality, in sales and service procedures, in spare parts supply, and in delivery reliability, could in turn enhance Soviet ability to earn the export revenue that would pay for these imports. The USSR has begun to open up its import and export channels along these lines. But how far will the authorities be willing to go? The potential benefits are accompanied by potential damages from volatile price changes and cyclical output fluctuations in the world economy; it will not be surprising if Soviet authorities proceed cautiously in expanding Soviet external economic relations during the 1980s.

ALTERNATIVE SOVIET PROSPECTS

The preceding chapters of this study have laid out in considerable detail the specific factor that are shaping the prospects for individual sectors of the Soviet economy. Moreover the computations with economywide models give general indications of how the economy as a whole is likely to perform over the next five or ten years. Beyond this, it may be useful in this concluding section to reflect in more qualitative terms, going outside the narrowly economic, on two possible types of Soviet evolution.

One would be the result of unchanged Soviet policies and unmodified Soviet institutions struggling to deal with the

174

objective developments that have been described in chapters 2 through 6. In dealing with these difficulties, Soviet authorities would continue applying the standard remedies of the past, in spite of their declining effectiveness. Strenuous campaigns to surmount obstacles and achieve priority targets would continue, leaving shortages and distortions in their wake, yet the rate of progress would be slower than in the past. In this "stand-pat scenario," the USSR would grow stronger and the Soviet people would improve their lot, but the quality of life would be widely perceived as unsatisfactory and the international standing of the USSR would not advance.

An interesting alternative to this "stand-pat scenario" would involve a series of reforms designed to remove the defects and break out of the dilemmas that have been sketched above. These would be the changes that might emerge from a new set of Party leaders, a group of reformers willing to make substantial changes in Soviet economic institutions. The specific improvements have all been suggested by Soviet economists over the last two decades, though the system has not been ready for them as long as adequate results were being obtained under orthodox procedures. The "reform scenario" is one that might unfold if the Party were to decide that present conditions require a new approach.

For this study, my co-authors and I have not computed a systematic set of outcomes under either "stand-pat" or "reform" assumptions, and it would be rash to offer sweeping generalizations without quantitative underpinning. But some of the basic contours of GNP trends and structure under these assumptions are clearly implied by previous analysis, so there is an adequate basis for a few limited statements. If present institutions remain unchanged, the rate of technological progress in the Soviet economy is likely to remain very slow. The USSR will make no headway in closing the gap between itself and Western Europe, Japan, and North America; in fact the gap may widen. Similarly there is not likely to be any fall in capital/output ratios. Declining capital productivity will combine with rising raw material costs to make labor productivity gains harder to realize. If present Soviet institutions remain unchanged, the agricultural sector will continue to perform badly, and its malperformance will hamper progress elsewhere in the economy. It will also at times endanger Soviet progress in foreign trade, whenever bad harvests lead to shortfalls that divert foreign exchange from nonagricultural imports. In the "stand-pat scenario" the USSR may even develop some trade debt problems, if years of high import needs coincide with periods of difficulty for Soviet exports. Finally, if Soviet policies remain unchanged, the share of GNP going to national defense by assumption remains unchanged. The absolute amounts of resources involved would presumably grow with the real GNP; this would apply both to manpower and to procurement of defense hardware.

By contrast with this, what would a "reform scenario" entail? Here the possibilities are legion and any answer must necessarily be more speculative. Again, however, drawing on available appreciations of the probable direction of specific reforms and crude estimates of how large the consequences might be, one can set down some reasonable predictions. First of all, if the incentive system is properly revised, if pressure for gross output is reduced, if the price system is administered less rigidly, and if operating decisions become more decentralized, the rate of Soviet technological progress is likely to rise perceptibly. Innovations would be adopted more speedily, production costs would be lowered, and product quality would be improved. There would probably be declines in capital/output ratios for industry and for agiculture, but if investment were directed more into housing and urban overhead capital (where capital/output ratios are always high), the capital/output ratio for the whole economy might not improve. A reformed and decentralized agriculture would surely perform more effectively than at present, though perhaps climatic difficulties would limit the gains. A reform-minded leadership would probably be willing to see Soviet links with the world economy grow stronger, and this in turn would probably improve the economy's performance, unless the outside world develops serious problems in the 1980s and the difficulties are transmitted to the USSR. Finally, a reform-minded leadership might reduce the defense share of GNP to spur general growth, as part of a set of policy changes designed to implement economic progress, and on the assumption that arms limitation agreements indicated no net reduction in Soviet national security. In such a "reform scenario," the USSR would by assumption make greater progress in solving its problems than under the "stand-pat scenario." Technological progress would be more rapid, resource use would be more efficient, living standards would rise more rapidly, and the USSR would gain greater international stature.

IMPLICATIONS OF SOVIET PROSPECTS FOR THE OUTSIDE WORLD

Since the USSR is a great power, her prospects have signficance for the world outside. Consider, for example, the possible implications for international relations if the "stand-pat" scenario is the one that unfolds over the next few years. Slow Soviet economic growth, accompanied by agricultural shortfalls and rising trade debts, would make the USSR a difficult trading partner. A domestic atmosphere of difficulties and dissatisfaction would engender poor morale and give rise to stern Party demands. Domestic dissidents would come under grim pressure. If the West were enjoying prosperous times the contrast with Soviet difficulties would make for abrasive relations. In all these tangible and intangible respects, a continuation of unchanged Soviet policies and institutions at home would radiate unfavorable consequences to the outside world.

By the same token, the external consequences of a "reform scenario" would be generally favorable. If there were enlarged scope for innovation and creativity in Soviet domestic affairs, the economy would of course become more efficient. If the reforms extended into the legal sphere, renewing the changes put through after Stalin died, the strength of domestic dissidence might abate, and gains in morale might lead to further gains in productivity. Domestic progress would make the USSR more confident and less defensive in international councils, not least because its economic relations would be on a stronger footing. Some might feel that the reforms smacked of "market socialism" or even "capitalism," but such a claim would reflect inadequate appreciation of Party doctrine. The USSR is currently in the process of moving toward "full communism," and the Party program adopted in 1961 provides ample grounds for claiming that the specific reforms in question fall very readily within its precepts.

There is very little, of course, that the outside world can do to influence the evolution of Soviet affairs. The selection of scenarios will depend on many factors, some completely beyond man's control and others forged by internal political processes that are mysteries to all but a handful of the Soviet Party leadership. In looking ahead at economic prospects, however, as we have done in this book, and in revising our judgments year by year as events unfold, it may nevertheless be helpful to have in mind these two broad scenarios as benchmarks against which to interpret emerging trends.